Sacraments: A Way of Life

Joyce Solimini
Author

Kieran Sawyer, S.S.N.D.
General Editor

Michael Amodei
Series Editor

Developing Faith
A Mini-Course Series for Teens

AVE MARIA PRESS Notre Dame, Indiana 46556

Nihil Obstat:
Reverend John R. Roos, J.C.D.
Censor Liborum

Imprimatur:
The Most Reverend Howard J. Hubbard, D.D.
Bishop of Albany

Given at Albany, NY on 31 May 1996

The *Nihil Obstat* and *Imprimatur* are official declarations that a book or pamphlet is free of doctrinal or moral error. No implication is contained therein that those who have granted the *Nihil Obstat* and *Imprimatur* agree with its contents, opinions, or statements expressed.

Some of the material in this book was previously published in *Developing Faith* by Sister Kieran Sawyer, copyright © 1978 by Ave Maria Press, Notre Dame, Indiana, Inc., *The Jesus Difference* by Sister Kieran Sawyer, copyright © 1987 by Ave Maria Press, Notre Dame, Indiana, and *The Risk of Faith* by Sister Kieran Sawyer, copyright © 1988 by Ave Maria Press, Notre Dame, Indiana.

International Standard Book Number: 0-87793-588-2

Cover and text design by Proof Positive/Farrowlyne, Inc.

Photography: Gene Plaisted, OSC 5; James L. Shaffer 31, 63, 84; Skjold Photographs 42, 95; Jim Whitmer Photography 20, 29, 52, 74, 106; W. P. Wittman 19.

Printed and bound in the United States of America.

Contents

Welcome

Dear Partners in Religious Education and Youth Ministry,

For years religious educators and youth ministers across the country have been asking me for an entire program based on the methodology found in my *Confirming Faith* sacramental preparation program and the *Tyme Capsule* retreat materials.

The *Developing Faith* mini-course series is an attempt to respond to that plea. Ave Maria Press has gathered a group of top-grade authors and youth practitioners to design with me a program for Catholic-Christian teens that will be engaging, comprehensive, flexible, and theologically sound, and that will involve the entire parish community in supporting the faith development of its adolescent members. I think you will find that a *Developing Faith* mini-course meets each of these criteria:

- Each course includes many dynamic interactive processes designed to *engage* teens' minds and hearts in thoughtful reflection, discussion, and prayer.
- The scope of the series is broad. *Developing Faith* offers mini-courses in all the crucial areas of religious literacy and formation. Enrichment and elective themes add to its *comprehensiveness.*
- The *flexibility* of the series is that it is made up of eight session courses that can be utilized in a variety of times and places in high school religious or youth ministry programs. A complete and easy-to-implement model for a parish faith development program has been provided.
- *Developing Faith* is *theologically sound.* Each course provides solid content in one or more aspects of the Catholic faith as outlined in the *Catechism of the Catholic Church.*

And finally, the *Developing Faith* mini-course series is built on the premise that the faith of adolescents grows best within a caring **faith community** made up of both youth and adults. The processes outlined in the program will help to form the teens and participating adults—catechists, group moderators, mentors, and parents—into a community that is truly Christian.

I encourage you to use the materials in this program creatively, courageously, and prayerfully. The transmission of the Christian faith from one generation to the next is a challenging and mysterious task, one in which God plays a much larger role than any of us. Let us pray together that the seeds of faith, planted at baptism in the hearts of our teens, will develop steadily and surely toward the fullness of Christian life.

Sincerely in Christ,

Sister Kieran Sawyer SSND

Sister Kieran Sawyer, SSND

Introduction

The *Developing Faith* Series in a Complete Faith Development Program

The *Developing Faith* series is designed to be the catechetical centerpiece of a comprehensive and flexible faith development program to, for, and by adolescents.

What is meant by a comprehensive and flexible faith development program? In general it is a program that mirrors much of the lifestyle of its participants. It is a program that can roll with a demanding teen schedule that might include basketball practice, a homecoming dance, and driver's training all in one week—yet still claim its rightful place of importance. (A comprehensive and flexible faith development program can likewise meet the varied interests and equally demanding schedules of adults who are asked to serve as catechists, as spiritual partners, and in other volunteer positions.) It is a program with lots of opportunities for free choices and various options. It is a program that recognizes that a fourteen-year-old ninth grader is developmentally much different than an eighteen-year-old senior. A comprehensive and flexible faith development program has many components—not just one or two. Evangelization, welcome, hospitality, prayer, worship, justice, service, mentoring, guidance, building relationships (among all members of the faith community, young and old), and fun are among its parts.

Why a comprehensive and flexible faith development program? A successful program must meet the needs of all its participants. As a consequence, a comprehensive and flexible faith development program offers *many* different times and places to attend, *many* ways to participate, *many* choices, and the opportunity for each person to freely decide what it is he or she needs and would like to learn, do, and be.

What is unique about the *Developing Faith* series? As the vehicle of religious education, the catechetical component of a comprehensive and flexible faith development program is of primary importance. The *Developing Faith* series offers courses in crucial areas of religious literacy and formation, including the scriptures, sacraments, and morality. However, its uniqueness is in its process. The material in *Developing Faith* includes the various kinds of activities that make up a successful faith development program—theological input, dialogue techniques, faith sharing, prayer experience, service opportunities, intergenerational participation—within each of the eight two to two-and-one-half hour sessions. Hence, participants in this *Sacraments: A Way of Life* mini-course experience in miniature the totality of a comprehensive and flexible faith development program.

The flexibility of the *Developing Faith* series also lends itself to many other faith-developing situations for adolescents. In part or whole, the session activities can be used as components for youth group meetings, religion classes, retreats, days of recollection, peer ministry meetings, small faith community gatherings, and so forth. Used in any of these ways, *Developing Faith* contributes to and is indeed a foundation for an expansive and engaging faith development program for youth.

A Model for Faith Development

Faith is fundamentally God's gift. It is God's personal offer of love and grace to each of us individually and to the community of believers we call church. Faith is also a human act. It is the response of trust, commitment, and submission that we make to God, both as individuals and as community.

The *Developing Faith* series is designed to help adolescent Christians develop the seeds of faith that were given to them at baptism. The *Rite of Baptism for Children* states that children who have been baptized as infants are to be brought up in such a way that they will gradually come to "accept for themselves" the faith in which they have been baptized (*RBC* 3).

Coming to accept the faith includes three distinct but interrelated processes: developing one's individual relationship with God, developing one's sense of belonging in a Christian community, and developing one's understanding of and allegiance to the institutional church. The *Developing Faith* series assists you, as catechist, to help the adolescents in your charge focus on each of these processes.

First, the program is designed to help young Christians to be aware of and responsive to the presence of God in their daily lives. It contains a variety of prayer and reflection exercises that guide the participants to grow in their understanding of the mysterious relationship between themselves and God, and to deepen their personal commitment to developing that relationship.

Second, the program is designed to help the participating group—adults and youth—to interact as a faith community where Christian values are shared and deepened. It helps the youth to appropriate the value system that guides the daily lives of the Christian community. It calls them to direct their lives according to the meaning system of a living community whose members' lives reflect the presence of Jesus. It invites them to accept for themselves the gift of living faith that resides in the Christian community.

And finally, the series is designed to help the adolescent participants choose to be active members of the institutional church with all that such membership implies. It helps them to understand and value the systems of rituals, writings, teachings, and moral directives that have been preserved and handed on through the church. It shows how the sacraments, creeds, and doctrines of the church help both the individual and the community to own, express, and deepen the gift of faith.

About the *Developing Faith* Series

A mini-course consists of eight two to two-and-one-half hour catechetical sessions on a variety of appropriate subjects for high-school religious education. The series is for religious education directors, youth ministers, catechists, teachers, and teenagers who are involved in a faith development program (i.e., youth ministry, religion class). The series is also for other adults from the local faith community who will join with the youth to provide a full experience of faith development.

Adult Participation

A mini-course can be conducted with any size group of teenagers, provided there is enough adult participation. An ideal size is thirty to forty teen participants, broken down into groups of six to eight.

The success of the faith development program is dependent on the participation of adults who take up various roles. Adult roles and their definitions are as follows:

Coordinator of the program

This person organizes the program and gets it started by contacting adult volunteers, inviting the teens, setting the calendar, arranging for the meeting place, and holding initial organizational meetings. (This person may be the DRE, youth minister, theology department chairperson, retreat director, or any other person charged with setting up a faith development program for teens.)

Director(s) of the session

This person studies the *Director's Manual,* prepares and teaches the sessions, directs the other activities, and gathers the materials needed for each session. It is helpful if the director has teaching experience.

Group moderators

Each moderator is assigned a group of about six to eight participants. This grouping—unlike the small discussion groups formed at each session—remains the same for the entire program. The moderators attend all the sessions if possible. They check the attendance of their groups, contact those who are absent or tardy, arrange for makeup work, check and record homework assignments and teen-mentor meeting summaries, arrange and moderate service opportunities, etc.

Mentors

Ideally, these are adults who are paired one-on-one with the teens. They attend some of the sessions and meet with the teens between sessions. In the individual teen-mentor meetings, the mentors dialogue with teens about issues raised in a session, work on activities together, socialize, have fun, and offer many other kinds of support. The mentors form a strong link between the teens and the adult faith community. More information on the spiritual mentoring concept is offered on pages 6–7 and in the *Mentor Handbook.*

Parents, relatives, adult friends, and neighbors of the teen participants

These persons are invited to attend as many sessions as possible. The ideal is to have at least one group moderator and one visiting adult present in each discussion group.

Total parish community

There are many ways to involve the entire parish community in a faith development program. Besides the roles mentioned above, parishioners may also serve as prayer partners (adults who pray for individual teens). Teens should be invited to attend and participate in functions of parish organizations. Occasional Sunday liturgies should be geared to teenage tastes and interests (with teens involved in the planning and various liturgical roles). Announcements at weekly liturgies should mention current courses and events being offered in the program.

Program Features

The *Developing Faith* series consists of the following components:

- *Director's Manual*
- *Participant Book*
- *Mentor Handbook*

The *Director's Manual* presents very detailed lesson plans, including a script for the input section of the sessions and directions for conducting all activities. The *Director's Manual* also lists the objectives for each session, an overview of the session content, a time estimation of the session sections, suggestions for the physical setting, and a detailed list of needed materials. One copy of the *Director's Manual* is needed for each person who will help to direct the sessions.

The sessions combine various kinds of process activities: theological input, dialoguing, faith sharing, and fun. Hence, the *Participant Book* is not a typical "read-around-the-room" text. Rather, it includes stories, surveys, questions, exercises, and prayers that flow from the sessions themselves. It also includes occasional home assignments and directions for meetings between the teen and the mentor. You will need one copy of the *Participant Book* for each participant, session director, group moderator, and several extra copies for use by the adults who attend the individual sessions. The mentors may also want their own copies of the *Participant Book*.

The *Mentor Handbook* includes an overview of the spiritual mentoring component of the program and a list of qualifications and requirements for mentors. One copy of the *Mentor Handbook* is needed for each mentor. The program coordinator should also keep a copy.

Settings

The mini-course sessions use a variety of settings. In an ideal situation all of the following kinds of spaces would be available. Of course, you will have to adapt to the space you have available:

Large-group presentation space

An area where the entire group can be seated on beanbag chairs, floor cushions, or chairs close to the director and the board.

Discussion tables

A space where the participants can meet in groups of six to eight, preferably around square or round tables. Long narrow cafeteria tables do *not* work for discussion groups because they spread the group out too far. If small tables are not available, form discussion groups without tables.

Cozy corners

Comfortable spaces where each of the small groups can gather. These spaces are often in the corners of the main large group room. Couches, beanbags, or floor cushions are helpful.

Prayer space

A comfortable area, preferably carpeted, large enough so the group can sit on the floor in a circle. It may be possible to use the church sanctuary for this part of the activities.

"Alone" spots

A space large enough for the participants to spread out for quiet times of individual prayer and reflection (but within voice and eye range of the director). The church, gym, or cafeteria works for this. A supply of cushions or carpet pieces is helpful.

Especially for smaller groups, certain sessions or parts of sessions may be conducted in the homes of either the adults or participants.

Eight Two to Two-and-One-Half Hour Sessions

Each mini-course includes eight sessions. Each session is designed to be used in a period that lasts for two to two-and-one-half hours. The eight sessions function best as a complete course. Though each session is self-contained, one lesson draws from the others. Each session includes fun and community-building activities, solid catechetical input, discussion techniques that help the participants assimilate the material presented, and an individual or group prayer experience. It is *possible* to use each session separately or segments of the material in shortened sessions, but the eight-session, two to two-and-one-half hour package has been created as a distinct unit and will be most effective when used as a whole.

About This Mini-Course

Sacraments: A Way of Life is a core subject mini-course in the area of Catholic sacraments and sacrament living. While series' introductions of this kind generally offer an overall breakdown of the specific sessions of a course, the *Developing Faith* team of authors has chosen to place this background information in the **Overview** panels for each session to allow for easier access when a session is being prepared for and used.

Additionally, the *Developing Faith* team, understanding the variety of background, skills and experiences of adolescents, refrains from offering a specific age recommendation for this course. This is a course that is accessible to a wide-range of adolescents in many different settings. Only you can determine if this mini-course is right for the adolescents in your group.

Mentor Concept

A distinct part of the *Developing Faith* series is the inclusion of the mentor component. In sum, a mentor is an adult from the local parish community who functions as a spiritual companion, adviser, counselor, and trusted friend to one or more candidates. The mentoring component is a tangible way for the adult members of the faith community to assist in the faith development of its adolescent members.

The mentor functions in this role in a series of informal one-on-one meetings with a teenager who is enrolled in the program. A detailed explanation of the qualifications and requirements of the mentor's role is presented in the *Mentor Handbook.*

Implementing the Mentoring Component

The mentoring component in a faith development program is ongoing. Here are some initial steps for implementation:

1. **Recruitment of Mentors** Announce the Mentor Information Meeting well in advance through the usual parish channels. Ask the teens to invite adults they know to the meeting.
2. **Mentor Information Meeting** Those interested in being mentors (and parents) are oriented to the mentoring concept and requirements at a Mentor

Information Meeting. After the meeting those who are still interested are interviewed and registered. Generally, one Mentor Information Meeting is held at the beginning of each program year and, if the numbers warrant it, the meeting can be repeated for new potential mentors and parents at the beginning of each block of mini-courses. (The complete Mentor Information Meeting plan is on pages 20-27).

3. **Pairing Teens and Mentors** After the meeting, the program coordinator and adult leaders finalize the pairings of teens and adults. A formal introduction of teens, parents, and mentors is arranged. It is recommended that the introductions take place at an informal reception held about thirty minutes prior to the first session.

4. **Teen-Mentor Meetings** One teen-mentor meeting plan with directions for conducting a meeting is included for each group session in the *Participant Book.* You may ask the teens and mentors to meet individually once between each session or once between every two sessions.

Messages to Mentors

The program coordinator or session director can communicate invitations to mini-course sessions, reminders about dates of upcoming events, specific activity assignments, and the like by asking the participants to write the message in the space titled "Mentor Memo" on the teen-mentor meeting page in the *Participant Book.*

Home Assignments

Home assignments are occasionally called for. Directions for some home assignments are given at the end of several sessions. At the teen-mentor meetings, the mentors are asked to choose one of three activities for the teen to complete. The activity itself or a written summary of what was done is checked by the group moderators at the next session.

How to Use the *Developing Faith* Series in a Complete Faith Development Program

The *Developing Faith* mini-courses are designed to fit comfortably into many different programming models. There is much freedom to adapt the mini-courses to many time-frames, settings, and existing academic calendars, or to use the mini-courses in a way that best meets the needs of your course or program.

Listed below are some ways to get started, common programming models, suggestions for scheduling, and other implementation and application notes.

Getting Started

An advantage of the eight-session mini-course is that you are more likely to be able to find adults to serve as session directors and moderators because of the shortened time commitment. To prepare adults to use the *Developing Faith* series in your parish, the following steps are recommended for the program coordinator:

1. Gather a group of interested adults to serve as group moderators. You will need one adult for every six to eight teen participants. It's better to approach volunteers through a personal network of connections in the parish rather than through a soliciting announcement in the parish bulletin. It is helpful if some of the volunteers have had experience in teaching or working with teenagers, but all do not need this background. What *is* needed is a love for teens.

2. Set up an organizational meeting for the adults. Share a presentation of the entire program based on the material found in this manual. This will provide the flavor of the program as well as the rationale. Other things for the program coordinator to do at this organizational meeting:
   - Ask each person to become familiar with the *Developing Faith* components: the *Director's Manual, Participant Book* and *Mentor Handbook*. Recommend that all read the introductory material in the *Director's Manual* for a thorough grounding in the theory and methodology of the program. Also recommend that they pay special attention to the Eight Be-Attitudes for Session Directors and Dialogue: Why and How sections in the Appendix, pages 118-121.
   - Decide on the director(s) for each session. It's best that one person serve as director for all eight sessions, though it is possible for more than one person to share the role.
   - Finalize as many dates as possible on the faith development program calendar. It is recommended that you schedule the Mentor Information Meeting several weeks before Session 1 to allow time to organize the adult leaders after they have experienced the method of this program in action.
   - Schedule a second organizational meeting, preferably after the Mentor Information Meeting.

3. Meet at a second organizational meeting. At the second organizational meeting the program coordinator should give directions for planning the subsequent sessions and other events. An agenda would include these tasks:
   - Assign each teen to a group moderator, who will check attendance, homework, service projects, and so forth for his or her group.
   - Decide how you will involve parents, mentors, and the total parish in the individual sessions. One simple method of assuring ongoing adult participation at the sessions is to make a list assigning each teen specific dates on which to bring an adult.
   - Plan a system of record keeping. It is important to have an accurate record of attendance, assignments completed, requirements fulfilled, etc. Records should be kept by the group moderators and turned over to the director at the end of the course.

Schedule and Content

One workable model is based on an academic year beginning in October and running through May. The year is divided into three eight-week trimesters and two four-week inter-terms.

Ideally, five or six mini-courses are offered each *trimester.* Mini-courses meet once a week at a variety of times and places. Service, social, and worship events (many in conjunction with the mentoring component) also take place. A sacramental preparation program weaves through the entire academic year.

During the *inter-terms* special events like teen retreats, service programs or projects, prayer services, and full- or half-day workshops on topics like sexuality or drug abuse are held.

The month of *September* is a time for registration, orientation, and information meetings.

The *summer months* are reserved for social events (camp outs, beach trips, and the like) and parish service projects (i.e., setting up a vacation Bible school for younger children), planning meetings, and vacation.

Youth Council

A youth council of twelve to fourteen high-school students from the parish with representatives from each grade is established. This group may be targeted and selected from recommendations from parents, teachers, pastoral staff, and other parishioners. The youth council meets regularly and works directly with the program coordinator and assistants to implement and maintain a total faith development program. Some of its tasks may include:

- helping to determine mini-course offerings (especially electives);
- developing, conducting, analyzing, and acting on the mini-course evaluations;
- arranging networking efforts between youth-sponsored programs and other programs within and outside of the parish;
- staffing and assisting at registration, workshops, service events, and retreats;
- surveying youth needs and suggesting ways to meet them;
- arranging and helping with social events like dances, camp outs, lock-ins, sports nights, amusement park trips, etc.

Requirements for Teens

Each participant may be required to take one, two, or three mini-courses (according to grade or age level) and one or more elective mini-course of his or her choice per year.

*What is a **required** mini-course?* The definition of a required mini-course can be determined by the program coordinator, adult assistants, and the youth council. Choices should be made on content and age-appropriateness. The following are just some examples of what may be required mini-course topics:

Jesus	Old Testament
Sacraments	New Testament
Reconciliation	Life Choices
Forming Conscience	Morality
Church History	Basic Beliefs

What is an ***elective*** *mini-course?* Elective mini-courses may explore a more specialized subject related to faith. Elective mini-courses are often based on the area of expertise or interest of the session directors. The program coordinator, adult assistants, and youth councils can survey the teens and the entire parish community for ideas about possible elective mini-courses. The following are just some of the examples of elective mini-course titles:

Exploring Religious Shrines in My Neighborhood
Images of God in the Star Trek Series
How Sports Parallel Religion
Composing Religious Music for Children
Comparing World Religions

Each participant is also required to attend two half-day workshops or one full-day workshop, one liturgical or prayer experience, and complete one major service project per year.

Sacrament Preparation

Preparation for the sacrament of confirmation is a part of many high-school faith development programs. Confirmation preparation adapts well to this model. The *Confirming Faith* program (Ave Maria Press, 1995), for example, includes twelve sessions. In an academic year divided into trimesters, sessions 1-4 are held in the first trimester, sessions 5-8 in the second trimester, sessions 9-12 in the third trimester. The sessions meet every two weeks. The inter-terms are used for retreats and service projects or to make adjustments in the overall schedule, for example, due to receiving an earlier confirmation date from the diocesan office.

The trimester model also lends itself to scheduling a religious-literacy course for teens who have received little or no religious training. This course can be used as a "catch-up" or review course for teens interested in receiving one or more of the initiation sacraments.

Any baptized person has the right to be confirmed. However, in order to ensure the integrity of the sacrament and the faith community, it is recommended that some basic catechetical prerequisites are observed. Many parishes require a *minimum* of one year's participation in a catechetical program before a candidate can begin immediate preparation for reception of a sacrament.

Sample Calendar

Listed on the next three pages is a sample calendar of a faith development program based on the trimester model. This list of courses (designated on the calendar by "MC") and activities is not exhaustive. Generally, three of the course offerings per trimester are required courses. The required courses as well as the number and titles of the electives can vary from trimester to trimester.

Fall Trimester

August

SUNDAY	MONDAY	TUESDAY	WEDNESDAY	THURSDAY	FRIDAY	SATURDAY
	1	2	3 Install new youth council and meet in first of regular monthly meetings; plan fall trimester schedule	4	5	6
7	8	9	10 Begin bulletin announcements for fall trimester	11	12	13
14	15	16	17 Continue ongoing youth social activities (sports nights, field trips, movies, roundtables, etc.)	18	19	20
21	22	23	24 Meet with fall trimester mini-course and session directors	25	26	27
28	29	30	31			

September

SUNDAY	MONDAY	TUESDAY	WEDNESDAY	THURSDAY	FRIDAY	SATURDAY
			Continue announcements for fall trimester (including Mentor Information Meeting and sacramental preparation)	1	2	3
4	5	6	7 Commission program directors and moderators at Catechetical Sunday liturgy	8	9	10
11	12	13	14 Register fall trimester participants (including confirmation preparation candidates)	15	16	17
18	19	20	21 Conduct orientation meetings (i.e., Confirmation Introductory Meeting and Mentor Information Meeting)	22	23	24
25	26	27	28 Continue ongoing youth meetings and activities	29	30	

October

SUNDAY	MONDAY	TUESDAY	WEDNESDAY	THURSDAY	FRIDAY	SATURDAY
						1
2 MC1 9:30 am MC2 6:00 pm	3 Youth Council	4 Confirmation Session 6:30 pm	5 MC3 7:00pm	6 MC4 7:00 pm MC5	7	8
9 MC1 9:30 am MC2 6:00 pm Rite of Welcome and Commitment	10 Open Gym	11	12 MC3 7:00pm	13 MC4 7:00 pm MC5	14	15 Lock-in
16 Lock-in Cont. MC1 9:30 am MC2 6:00 pm	17 Movie Night	18 Confirmation Session 6:30 pm	19 MC3 7:00pm	20 MC4 7:00 pm MC5	21	22
23 MC1 9:30 am MC2 6:00 pm	24 Open Gym	25	26 MC3 7:00pm	27 MC4 7:00 pm MC5	28	29
30 MC1 9:30 am MC2 6:00 pm	31 Halloween Trick or Treating					

November

SUNDAY	MONDAY	TUESDAY	WEDNESDAY	THURSDAY	FRIDAY	SATURDAY
		1	2 MC3 7:00pm	3 MC4 7:00 pm MC5	4	5
6 MC1 9:30 am MC2 6:00 pm	7 Youth Council	8 Confirmation Session	9 MC3 7:00pm	10 MC4 7:00 pm MC5	11	12
13 MC1 9:30 am MC2 6:00 pm	14 Open Gym	15	16 MC3 7:00pm	17 MC4 7:00 pm MC5	18	19 Hay Ride
20 MC1 9:30 am MC2 6:00 pm	21 Movie Night	22 Confirmation Session	23 MC3 7:00pm	24 Thanksgiving Dinner for Homeless and Poor	25	26
27	28 Open Gym	29	30			

December

SUNDAY	MONDAY	TUESDAY	WEDNESDAY	THURSDAY	FRIDAY	SATURDAY
				1 MC4 7:00 pm MC5	2	3
4 "Giving Tree" Service Project	5 Youth Council	6	7	8	9 Weekend	10 Retreat
11 "Giving Tree" Service Project Weekend Retreat	12 Open Gym	13 Infancy Narrative Seminar Part I 7:00pm	14	15 Infancy Narrative Seminar Part II 7:00pm	16	17 Christmas Dance
18 "Giving Tree" Service Project	19	20	21 Free Babysitting for Christmas Shoppers	22 Christmas Caroling	23	24 Youth Mass
25	26	27 Sexuality Seminar Part I 7:00pm	28	29 Sexuality Seminar Part II 7:00pm	30	31 New Years Eve Lock-In

Interterm

January

SUNDAY	MONDAY	TUESDAY	WEDNESDAY	THURSDAY	FRIDAY	SATURDAY
1	2 Youth Council	3 ← Registration	4 for Winter	5 Trimester →	6	7
8 MC1 6:00 pm	9 Open Gym	10 Confirmation Session	11 MC2 7:00 pm MC3	12 MC4 7:00 pm	13 Horror Movie Lock-In	14 MC5 9:00 am
15 MC1 6:00 pm	16 Movie Night	17	18 MC2 7:00 pm MC3	19 MC4 7:00 pm	20	21 MC5 9:00 am
22 MC1 6:00 pm	23 Open Gym	24 Confirmation Session	25 MC2 7:00 pm MC3	26 MC4 7:00 pm	27	28 MC5 9:00 am
29 MC1 6:00 pm	30 Pizza Bash	31				

Winter Trimester

February

SUNDAY	MONDAY	TUESDAY	WEDNESDAY	THURSDAY	FRIDAY	SATURDAY
			1 MC2 7:00 pm MC3	2 MC4 7:00 pm	3	4 MC5 9:00 am
5 MC1 6:00 pm	6 Youth Council	7 Confirmation Session	8 MC2 7:00 pm MC3	9 MC4 7:00 pm	10	11 MC5 9:00 am Valentine's Day Progressive Dinner
12 MC1 6:00 pm	13	14 Fat Tuesday Ice Cream Party	15 MC2 7:00 pm MC3 Ash Wednesday Service 5:00 pm	16 MC4 7:00 pm	17	18 MC5 9:00 am
19 MC1 6:00 pm	20	21 Confirmation Session	22 MC2 7:00 pm MC3	23 MC4 7:00 pm	24 Soup Supper Sponsor 6:00pm	25 MC5 9:00 am
26 MC1 6:00 pm	27	28				

Winter Trimester

March

SUNDAY	MONDAY	TUESDAY	WEDNESDAY	THURSDAY	FRIDAY	SATURDAY
			1 MC2 7:00 pm MC3	2 MC4 7:00 pm	3	4 MC5 9:00am
5	6 Youth Council	7	8 Seminar: The Passion of Jesus 6:00 pm	9	10 Ski	11 Trip
12 Ski Trip Cont.	13 Open Gym	14	15	16	17 Soup Supper Sponsor 6:00 pm	18 Day Workshop: Drug Awareness 10:00 am
19	20 Meeting for Next Year's Youth Council Candidates	21	22 Communal Reconciliation Service	23	24 Confirmation	25 Retreat
26 Clothing Canned Food Drive Ends	27 ←	28	29 Holy Week	30 Holy Thursday Mass of the Lord's Supper	31 Good Friday Living Stations of the Cross Presentation →	

Interterm

Spring Trimester

April

SUNDAY	MONDAY	TUESDAY	WEDNESDAY	THURSDAY	FRIDAY	SATURDAY
						1
2 Easter	3 Youth Council	4 Confirmation Session	5	6	7	8
9 Rite of Acceptance	10 Volleyball League	11 MC1 7:00pm MC2	12 MC3 6:00pm	13 MC4 7:00pm MC5	14	15 Amusement Park Trip
16	17 Trivial Pursuit Tournament	18 MC1 7:00pm MC2 Confirmation Session	19 MC3 6:00pm	20 MC4 7:00pm MC5	21	22
23 / 30	24 Volleyball League	25 MC1 7:00pm MC2	26 MC3 6:00pm	27 MC4 7:00pm MC5	28	29

← Registration for Spring Trimester → (April 2–8)

May

SUNDAY	MONDAY	TUESDAY	WEDNESDAY	THURSDAY	FRIDAY	SATURDAY
	1 Youth Council	2 MC1 7:00pm MC2 Confirmation Session	3 MC3 6:00pm	4 MC4 7:00pm MC5	5	6
7	8 Volleyball League	9 MC1 7:00pm MC2	10 MC3 6:00pm	11 MC4 7:00pm MC5 Ascension Day	12	13 Family Reconciliation Service
14 Mother's Day Buffet Youth Council Election	15 Movie Night	16 MC1 7:00pm MC2 Confirmation Session	17 MC3 6:00pm	18 MC4 7:00pm MC5	19 Confirmation Rehearsal	20 Sacrament of Confirmation
21 Youth Council Election Pentecost	22 Volleyball League	23 MC1 7:00pm MC2	24 MC3 6:00pm	25 MC4 7:00pm MC5	26 Christian Service Projects Due	27
28	29	30 MC1 7:00pm MC2	31 MC3 6:00pm			

← Campaigning for Youth Council → (May 7–13)

June

SUNDAY	MONDAY	TUESDAY	WEDNESDAY	THURSDAY	FRIDAY	SATURDAY
				1	2	3
4	5	6	7	8	9	10
11	12	13	14	15	16	17
18	19	20	21	22	23	24
25	26	27	28	29	30	

Week 1: Last sessions of mini-courses

Week 2: After Confirmation session

Week 3: Sponsor Vacation Bible School for primary children

Week 4: Evaluate year's programs

Week 5: Continue regularly scheduled events (i.e., gym night, movie night, etc.)

July

SUNDAY	MONDAY	TUESDAY	WEDNESDAY	THURSDAY	FRIDAY	SATURDAY
						1
2	3	4	5	6	7	8
9	10	11	12	13	14	15
16	17	18	19	20	21	22
23 / 30	24 / 31	25	26	27	28	29

Week 2: Last meeting of current Youth Council

Week 3: Catechetical training and enrichment

Week 4: Plan next academic year's mini-courses; search for volunteers

Week 5: Conduct major social and service events (i.e., camp outs, beach trips, Habitat for Humanity, etc.)

Using the *Developing Faith* Series in Other Models and Settings

Flexibility is a main feature of the *Developing Faith* series. Using an eight-session course is not limited to the trimester model. Here are brief descriptions of some other models:

Sixteen-week semester course in a parish faith development program.

Schedule one session every two weeks. Assign teen-mentor meetings in the alternate weeks.

Eight-week quarter course in a parish faith development program.

Schedule mini-courses similar to the trimester model. Eliminate the interterms. The academic calendar would include four quarters running from October through May.

Sixteen-week semester course in a school setting.

Eliminate the opening activity. In the first week, reserve one class period to do Part I of the session. In the second week, reserve a second class period to do Part II of the session. Continue over a sixteen-week semester. The process-style lesson can provide a break from more traditional teaching methods used during the rest of the week. The mini-course material can be used to supplement or enrich the rest of the school course.

Eight-week quarter course in a school setting.

Divide the mini-course session into three approximately fifty-minute sections. Use the sections on a Monday-Wednesday-Friday basis in class.

Mini-workshop or retreat.

The mini-course subject matters can be used as the main themes of a mini-workshop or retreat. The session plans can be abridged to fit the specific time frame.

Advance Preparation

Long-term planning is helpful for whatever programming model is chosen. All eight session plans should be previewed by the session director(s). Supply lists should be compiled, music and video ordered, settings arranged, and special preparations made prior to the start of the course.

Orientation Meeting

Mentor Information Meeting

Objectives

The purpose of the Mentor Information Meeting is to gather potential adults who are interested in the role of the mentor:

- to share with them the model of faith that is the basis of this faith development program;
- to present the qualifications and requirements of the mentoring role;
- to conduct one-on-one interviews with the potential mentors and mutually decide if the role of mentor is for them.

Overview

This meeting is designed to allow interested adults a taste of the process-style the teens will experience in each mini-course session. A faith-sharing activity, a large group presentation, and a prayer experience are the main parts of the meeting. The adults are introduced to the faith model at the core of this series: the three aspects of faith (personal, communal, and institutional) and how the faith reality is nourished by caring members of the faith community throughout the long journey of life. This meeting also explains more about what being a mentor for a teen entails. Those who are sufficiently interested in becoming mentors are then individually interviewed to mutually determine whether or not this role is for them. The interviewers and program coordinator gather after the interviews to share their information, determine a roster of mentors, and match unattached teens with adults on the list.

Session Outline

I. Who Are Mentors? (about 40 minutes)
II. Model of Faith (about 15 minutes)
III. Prayer Experience (about 15 minutes)
IV. Break (about 5 minutes)
V. The Mentoring Component—More Information (about 15 minutes)
VI. Questions and Answers (about 10 minutes)
VII. Interviews (about 20 minutes)

Supplies

You will need the following supplies:

- name tags
- a schedule with times and dates of important events in the program
- newsprint (one large sheet for each table)
- markers (one set for each table)
- copies of the Mentor Handbook
- pencils
- recording of instrumental background music (optional)
- copies of Resource 1, the Mentor Interview and Registration Form
- a few copies of the Participant Book for each interview station

Special Preparations

At the end of the meeting, a time is reserved for those interested in being a mentor to be interviewed. Orient an interview team to (1) conduct interviews and (2) offer input into the pairing of teens with adult mentors. One interviewer (pastor, parents, pastoral staff) is needed to interview every four adults interested in being a mentor.

Setting

You will need the following areas for this meeting:

1. An area where the participants can meet around tables in groups of about eight.
2. An area where you can gather all the participants for the presentations. Arrange the chairs around a podium and chalkboard.
3. A large open area where everyone can gather in a circle for prayer.
4. An area for one-on-one interviews. A writing surface (either a table or clipboard) is needed for each interview area. There should be enough space between interview areas for privacy.
5. A hospitality area with coffee and refreshments.

I. Who Are Mentors?

(about 40 minutes)

Welcome

1. Moderators welcome the participants as they arrive, ask them to make their name tags, and distribute copies of the Mentor Handbook. The participants are directed to the small group tables. When everyone has arrived, formally welcome the group and thank them for coming. Present a talk based on the following material as it corresponds to pages 7-14 of the Mentor Handbook.

Definitions and Examples

2. Briefly overview the mentoring concept, either from the Greek legend or as the concept applies to your program. Concretize the examples of mentors listed on pages 7-8 by sharing stories (from your own experience or those of teens you have worked with) of mentors you know who are:

   Teachers
   Tell about a teacher who influenced you in your teen years or about a teen you know who was encouraged to develop his or her interests and talents at the direction of a teacher.

   Coaches
   Under this category fall mentors who inspire an appreciation of teamwork as individuals join together to work for a common goal. Tell about an athletic coach, drama teacher, band leader, or another person you know who has had great success working with teens.

   Older Relatives
   Good listening is an unappreciated yet vital skill. Many teens have adult relatives (other than mom or dad) who they can talk with about anything. Sometimes neighbors, family friends, and others in the parish family fill this role. Share a story you know about an adult who provides a nonjudgmental ear to a teen and the positive effect the person has had on the teen's life.

3. Briefly explain how the traditional role of a Christian sacramental sponsor is similar to that of a mentor's role (see Mentor Handbook, pages 9-11) and how a goal of this program is to return to the original concept of Christian sponsorship.

4. Overview how the teen-mentor relationship will function in the context of the faith development program (see Mentor Handbook, page 11) and the general characteristics of the teens who are enrolled in your program (see pages 11-13). Say:

   > Faith sharing is an essential part of this program, both in the class sessions and in the individual meetings between teens and mentors. The program is based on two fundamental principles of the *National Catechetical Directory:* (1) that total catechesis always includes sharing in the faith-life of a community; and (2) that the entire parish community is responsible for the catechesis of its members.

5. Point out the qualifications and requirements of a mentor in your program (see Mentor Handbook, pages 13-14).

Faith Sharing

6. Pass out a piece of newsprint and a set of markers to each table group. Take the participants through the reflection questions on page 9 of the Mentor Handbook. Say:

   > Who was a classroom teacher who was influential in your teen years? Write the person's name and a word to describe an important lesson he or she taught you. (Pause.)

Who was an athletic coach, drama teacher, band leader, scout master (et al.) who encouraged you to develop and perfect an individual talent? Write his or her name and the name of the talent that was perfected. (Pause.)

Who was an older relative or other adult you knew as a teen who you could count on for advice and to be a wise but non-judgmental friend? Write his or her name and a word to describe some wisdom that he or she imparted to you. (Pause.)

Now please share with your group why your teacher was so influential. The person with the biggest watch can begin. Then go around the circle again and tell about how your talent was perfected with the help of a special coach. Finally share something of the wisdom you learned from an older relative or other adult when you were a teen. (Allow a few minutes for sharing, then continue.)

You are no longer a teen-ager. You are an adult who has already—if you think about it—been a mentor for others. Now you are considering providing the same kind of support to a teen in this program. Write the names of three teens you have mentored and the particular role (teacher, coach, relative) you had next to each name.

Tell your group about one of these experiences of mentoring. The person wearing the most blue can go first.

II. Model of Faith

(about 15 minutes)

Ask the participants to focus their attention on the chalkboard. Summarize the material covered to this point. Say:

Besides being a teacher, coach, or good listener, a mentor is a **model** (write) of how a person of faith lives in today's world; a **friend** (write) who comes to know the teen and the teen's maturing faith; a **guide** (write) who is also a confidant and listener; a **learner** (write) who is also interested in his or her own growing faith; and a **spiritual companion** (write) who shares prayer time with the teen and helps the teen to understand and accept the gift of faith. In this program, the adult mentor helps the teen to grow in faith in each of three closely related but very different aspects. These aspects are represented by the diagram on page 15 of the Mentor Handbook.

(Draw the faith model on the board. If some of the group are familiar with the model from other presentations, ask them to explain the three aspects of faith represented by the diagram. If the diagram is new to the group, or if you want to expand on the participants' explanations, proceed with an explanation based on the text on pages 14-16 of the Mentor Handbook or on page 7 of this manual.)

III. Prayer Experience

(about 15 minutes)

1. Ask the participants to form a circle in a large group meeting space. (It would be preferable for the participants to sit on chairs; however, if this is not possible sitting on a carpeted floor will do.) Place a lighted candle in the center of the circle. Have one of the adult moderators start the musical accompaniment (live or on tape). Darken the room. Then, lead a prayer based on the following script.

Prayer Script

2. To illustrate the role of mentor as one who shares prayer, let us offer our own prayers of petition and thankfulness.

   Recall the stick person in the center of the faith model diagram that represents our personally experienced faith. Our awareness of God is a personal gift, contingent upon awareness of self and of reality. If you had to choose a way you most often experience the presence of God, what would it be? Witnessing a beautiful sunset? In the midst of personal tragedy? When a particular song plays on the radio? When you are with someone you love? Take a moment and reflect on a way you experience God's presence. Then share your way with the person sitting next to you. (Allow time for the reflection and sharing, then continue.)

   The Christian community—recall the wavy line on the diagram—struggles to live faith day by day. Accepting the living faith of a Christian community is a process of absorbing the values and meanings which the group espouses. The more vibrant the faith of the community and the more it informs the actions and decisions of the members, the more readily its faith is accepted by children, youth, and all initiates. We pray for our local faith community at name of parish (mention a need of the parish-at-large; for example, "a room to store food and clothing for our social justice outreach" or "for a successful semester in our religious education program") and respond, "Lord, hear our prayer."

   (Offer the participants the opportunity to pray for a need of the parish community or to offer thanks for a grace received by the community. Allow time for these individual prayers, then continue.)

   Accepting the formal faith system of the church—the outside circle—means coming to understand the meaning of the symbols, rituals, doctrines, and laws in which the faith has been expressed. It is a process of learning to delve beneath these symbols to discover the deeper faith realities they represent. We pray for our universal church (mention a need; for example, "for the pope" or "for an increase of vocations to the priesthood or religious life . . .") and respond, "Lord, hear our prayer."

(Offer the participants the opportunity to pray for a need of the universal church or to offer thanks for a grace present in the universal church. Allow time for these individual prayers, then continue.)

God, we your people offer these prayers from our heart.
We ask that you remember the adults who have come here tonight.
Inspire them in the task of modeling their faith to others.
Help them to serve the role of mentor well.
We pray also for the youth in our faith development program and for their families.
We pray in Jesus' name.
Amen.

IV. Break

(about 5 minutes)

Take a five-minute break. Have the group stretch and move the chairs (if necessary) back to their positions for a large group presentation.

V. The Mentoring Component— More Information

(about 15 minutes)

1. Ask the group to bring their Mentor Handbook to the large group meeting area. Pass out copies of the faith development program schedule. When everyone is ready, continue an overview of the mentoring component based on the material in the Mentor Handbook. Add explanation as needed for each of the points that follow.

The Teen-Mentor Meeting

2. Provide details about the date, time, and place of the formal introduction between the teen and mentor. Ideally, this formal introduction would take place at a reception prior to the first mini-course session (see page 32). At the time of the formal introduction, the teens and mentors exchange phone numbers and arrange the dates, times, and places of some or all of their meetings.

   Explain how often you will require the teens and mentors to meet.

   Point out that teen-mentor meeting plans are included with each session in the Participant Book. Go over the basic format as outlined on pages 17-19 of the Mentor Handbook.

Effective Communication

3. Read the foundational points of the dialogue process (see Mentor Handbook, pages 19-20). Expand on each point as necessary.

Mentoring More Than One Teen

4. Cover the section on pages 20-21 of the Mentor Handbook as it applies to your program.

Group Events

5. Explain that special events like attending sessions, social outings and retreats, working on service projects, and participating in liturgical events will be periodically required. If applicable, refer to any of these events already on the schedule.

   Optional: Arrange for an adult and teen from last year's mentor program to share their reflections, comments, and observations about the experience.

VI. Questions and Answers

(about 10 minutes)

Allow about ten minutes for questions from the participants.

VII. Interviews

(about 20 minutes)

1. While the group is still in the presentation area, briefly explain the purpose of the individual interviews. Say:

> If you remain interested in becoming a mentor for one or more of the youth in this program, we ask that you meet now with one of the adult team members at one of the interview stations. (Point them out.) We will be able to dialogue more about the qualifications and expectations of the mentoring program. We will answer any questions you still have. We will ask if you have been invited here by a specific teen or if you are open to being assigned to a teen who does not have a mentor. We will go over the first mentor meeting plan with you in more detail.
>
> While you are waiting for your interview, please enjoy coffee and refreshments. You may leave after your interview. Thank you for coming and we will see many of you again on _________ (mention the dates of the first mini-course sessions or other initial meeting dates you have scheduled for mentors, teens, and parents).

A host or hostess (maybe a teen from the Youth Council) can direct the participants to the refreshment table.

Interview Format

2. The interviewer is to conduct the interview in the following manner:

   Greet the person and ask him or her to fill in the first lines on the Mentor Interview and Registration Form (Resource 1). If applicable, also have the interviewee write the name of the teen who invited him or her to the meeting. Then, ask one or more of the following questions (jot notes on the registration form):

   - How did you hear about this meeting?
   - What interests you about being a mentor?
   - What recent experiences relating to teens have you had?
   - How do you feel you meet each qualification for the mentor role? (See page 13 of the Mentor Handbook.)
   - How able are you to meet the requirements of the program? (See pages 13-14 of the Mentor Handbook.)

3. Refer to the Participant Book. Turn to pages 13-14, Teen-Mentor Meeting 1, and allow the interviewee the chance to examine its content. Ask if he or she has any questions. Explain as needed.

4. Remind him or her that at the end of each teen-mentor meeting the mentor is to sign and date the meeting verification section included for each session in the Participant Book.

5. Conclude the interview. Say:

   You will be contacted by phone with further instructions and information. Thank you very much.

After the Meeting

6. The members of the interview team turn in their copies of the Mentor Interview and Registration Form. Discuss specific comments.

7. Work together to pair teens and mentors.

8. Contact the mentors by telephone and/or mail about the first mini-course session (or other formal meeting date and time).

9. Call any adults you have not chosen to be mentors, for whatever reason. Thank them for their interest. Tell them their names will be kept on file.

Group Sessions

Sacraments: A Way of Life

session One

Objectives

The purpose of this session is to help the participants:

- appreciate sacramentality as a way of seeing life;
- name some sacramental experiences in their own lives;
- understand the sacramental actions of the church as a continuation of Jesus' life and ministry.

Overview

A uniqueness of Catholic Christianity is its sacramental tradition. Catholics have always revered God's presence in the ordinary "stuff" of human life: in creation, in the movements of nature, in relationships, in meal-sharing, in moments of healing and reconciliation, and in the natural rhythms of "little deaths" and "little resurrections." A sacramental view of life acknowledges that God has taken the initiative to enter fully into human life and that we have the capacity to recognize and respond to God in every aspect of our lives. Jesus himself modeled a sacramental spirituality as he pointed out the tangible signs of the reign of God. The trust of sparrows and of children, the sharing of meals with sinners, sowing seeds and casting nets, healing pools and stormy waters, the touches of healing and reconciliation: all spoke loudly of the faithfulness of a loving God who is able to transform us. In this session, the participants have a chance to "try on" this sacramental view of life, which was Jesus' way of seeing. The opening activity explores the many different ways that people can look at life. Part I covers in more detail names for the various perspectives people carry, including, optimists, pessimists, escapists, seekers, and visionaries. A scripture activity helps the participants explore different perspectives of the gospel stories. In Part II, the participants examine more closely Jesus' way of seeing and the things in life that Jesus considered important. The participants see how the essential reminders of the life and ministry of Jesus have been designated by the church as the seven sacraments.

Mentor Component

It is recommended that you invite the mentors, teens, and parents to a brief hospitality reception about thirty minutes before the start of this session to provide an opportunity for formal introductions. Plan to invite the mentors and/or parents to stay for the first session (optional). Preview the Teen-Mentor Meeting 1 plan on pages 13-14 of the Participant Book.

Session Outline

Opening Activity: Lenses on Life (about 20 minutes)

Part I: Jesus' Lens on the World (about 50 minutes)

Break (about 5 minutes)

Part II: The Church Continues Jesus' Way of Seeing (about 50 minutes)

Prayer Experience: Gifted with the Eyes of Faith (about 15 minutes)

Feedback and Conclusion (about 10 minutes)

Supplies

For this session you will need:

- pencils or pens
- extra copies of the Participant Book
- a "blurred" op-art drawing
- two small display tables
- large tablecloth or linen
- various kinds of glasses/lenses (see Opening Activity, No. 2)
- a large mirror
- bibles (one for each participant)
- personal mementos from the session director's life (e.g., family photos, class ring, Christmas ornament, special gift, heirloom, souvenir of travel, etc.)
- newsprint
- markers
- VCR and monitor
- *Jesus of Nazareth* (Franco Zefferelli production) or other video that depicts a portion of Jesus' ministry
- (optional) a poster depicting one or more events of Jesus' ministry
- several mementos depicting Jesus' life, words, and ministry (e.g., an old sandal, an old coin, perfume, a cloth bandage, a loaf of bread, a small seed, a crutch, a cross, etc.)
- candle
- bowl of holy water
- CD or tape player
- tape

Special Preparations

1. Find a news story about a contemporary person who through his or her behavior can be described as an escapist (e.g., drug abuser, participator in manipulative sexual relationship, suicide victim). Plan to share the story and show an accompanying article or photo.
2. Cue the video to a segment (ten minutes maximum) which helps them to recall a particular event of Jesus' ministry: his baptism, the wedding at Cana, healing stories, the feeding of the multitudes, a meeting with a public sinner, or the commissioning of Peter and/or the disciples.
3. Prepare a teen to slowly, reverently read the passage from John 9:1-11 for the Prayer Experience.

Settings

You will need the following areas for this session:

1. A large area where the participants can gather in a relaxed and comfortable atmosphere for large-group discussions. The room should have an open space from which the participants can easily view a chalkboard or easel. Prepare two tables in the large meeting area before the participants arrive. On one table, place the assortment of lenses you have collected (see Opening Activity, No. 2). On the second table, place the mementos you have collected from your life. Cover the memento table with a cloth so that the items cannot been seen until the cloth is removed.
2. An area where teens can gather around circular tables in groups of six to eight.
3. A hospitality area to share snack foods and drinks (optional).
4. "Alone" spots—places where the participants can be at least six feet away from everyone else.
5. An area for the Prayer Experience. The floor of the church sanctuary often works well. If this area is impossible to use, arrange the large group area into a comfortable setting for prayer. Place a cloth on the floor. Display a bowl of water, a candle, and an enthroned bible on the cloth. Set up the tape or CD player and cue the recording you have chosen.

Opening Activity: Lenses on Life

(about 20 minutes)

Welcome

1. Greet the participants and direct them to the large meeting area. When everyone has arrived, ask them to gather around the table you have set up with lenses. Take a survey by hands on how many people have ever used one or more of the lenses on the table. Then, put on a pair of sunglasses and ask:

What are these glasses for? (Pause to elicit responses; e.g., to block the sun, to disguise one's appearance, to be "cool.") Who are people that might wear them (e.g., baseball players, drivers, sunbathers, etc.)

2. Pass the sunglasses to one of the teens and ask him or her to wear them for the rest of the discussion. Then continue using the same questions for the other lenses on the table. Elicit responses like the following for the various types of lenses. Don't forget to assign a teen to wear the lenses as you proceed with the discussion.

   Sample Responses

   - Bifocals give two "perspectives." They are worn by people who want to "balance their vision."
   - Rose-colored glasses shade everything one color. They are worn by people who want to see the world in a new tint, have fun, or be in fashion.
   - Virtual reality specs put a person "in the scene" and make everything appear three-dimensional. They are worn by people who like to feel involved.
   - Binoculars bring faraway things up close. They are used by people at sporting or theater events or sometimes by people who want to spy on others.
   - Magnifying glasses highlight minuscule details of a larger objects. They are used by scientists, criminalists, and the like.
   - Blindfolds block out sight. They are worn by people who are playing a game and decide to give up their sight temporarily.
   - "Groucho" glasses with nose and mustache provide a touch of humor. They are worn by people who want to be laughed at or make others laugh.

3. After you've briefly introduced each of the lenses, allow all the participants to take turns trying the pairs on and looking at themselves in the mirror. Then assign each participant to an adult moderator (approximately six to eight participants in each group) and ask them to move to a small-group table. Explain that the adult moderator is the person the participants will report to each session for keeping attendance records, verifying teen-mentor meeting summaries, and checking homework assignments. Call on a runner from each table to distribute bibles, pens or pencils, and copies of the Participant Book to each person in their group.

4. After everyone is at a table, ask them to open their books to page 8, "My Lens on Life." Tell them to use the scale to mark each of the items. Allow a brief time for marking. Then ask them to go around the table and share the item with the highest number and a clarifying statement to explain why they view themselves this way. The person in the group wearing the largest glasses can go first.

Part I: Jesus' Lens on the World

(about 50 minutes)

1. Have the participants remain at their tables. Make sure that everyone is able to view a chalkboard or easel. Introduce the topic by reading or summarizing the introductory text on page 7 of the Participant Book. You may wish to call on volunteers to comment on the Rio de Janeiro example. Continue the discussion on particular "lenses on life" with a presentation based on the following script.

Script

2. Whether people wear glasses or not, we all have a "lens" on life, a perspective through which we view life. For example, some people are **optimists** (write). There is even a saying that optimists see life through "rose-colored glasses." Usually, an optimist is someone we enjoy being around. They are encouraging and hopeful people. They seem to be able to find something good in every situation and turn even the most dire experiences into something positive. When you hear the word "optimist," who do you think of? Take turns going around the table and tell why you view this person as an optimist and how this person has had an influence on you. The person wearing the most rose or red goes first. (Allow time for everyone to share.)

   Other people are **pessimists** (write). We might describe them as "sunglasses types" who always see the dark side of life. Pessimists are people who automatically gravitate to a negative in any situation. For example, pessimists are the ones who looks at the half-filled glass as being "half empty." They rarely laugh or smile. Pessimists cannot be happy in a good situation and they make a bad situation worse by their attitude. Think about a time when you carried a pessimistic attitude. How did it affect your experience? Share this incident with your group. This time the person wearing the most blue goes first. (Allow time for sharing.)

   Escapists (write) are people who, at least symbolically, wear blindfolds through life. They don't want to deal with reality. They run away from any situation that is the least bit threatening. A problem with this way of living is that escapists are seldom challenged by new experiences that might allow them to grow and better themselves as people. More seriously, in avoiding difficult situations, escapists sometimes find hiding places in dangerous things like alcohol or drugs, manipulative relationships, acquisition of possessions. (Share a story of a contemporary person who you consider an "escapist" accompanied by a news article or photo.)

   Some people are **seekers** (write), "magnifying glass" people who want to experience every detail in the adventure they call life. Seekers are usually not satisfied with the way things are. They are always asking questions, especially "why?" Seekers are open to new relationships, new opportunities, new paths in life. Seekers are not afraid to take risks that would help them grow as persons. Seekers keep questioning and moving forward more for the satisfaction of the journey itself rather than for any rewards they might find. Think of someone who is a seeker. How has this person influenced you? Share with your group. The person with the most neatly combed hair goes first. (Allow time for sharing.)

(Display a "blurred" op-art drawing near the board or easel. Call a volunteer to come forward and attempt to make out the image by squinting his or her eyes. If the person is unable to do so, call a few more volunteers to try before you tell them what the image depicts.) **Visionaries** (write) are people who have the ability to see beyond what meets the eye. Visionaries see ordinary things in extraordinary ways. Visionaries tend to look at the deeper meanings of life. They help everyone to appreciate life and one another. They call us to awaken our senses when they have been dulled. They help us to see the writing on the wall, to pick out the clues in life so that we can focus more clearly on what is really important. Jesus was a visionary. He helped people see that the reign of God was at hand for those with "eyes to see."

Scripture Exercise

3. Ask the participants to turn to page 9, "The Jesus Lens." Introduce the exercise. Say:

   As we just heard, people view life in many different ways. A great part of Jesus' mission was to lead people to view the seemingly ordinary words and actions of life—conflicts, hospitality, shared meals, reconciliation—from a new perspective, to see things as being "charged" with the presence of God.

4. Read the exercise directions. Have the participants work in pairs to look up and read the scripture passages. Ask the group moderators to help the participants locate the passages in the Bible if necessary. Tell them they can share and compare answers, but they should each write their own answers in the space provided. Allow about ten minutes for work on the exercise. Then, go over the answers below:

   Answers

   1. Through his baptism, Jesus identified himself with sinners. He also left an example for others to follow and showed that God was present at his baptism.
   2. Jesus counted the outcasts of society—tax collectors and sinners—among his friends and often ministered to them at table.
   3. The sellers and moneychangers were in the Temple to help the Jews fulfill a part of the law that required them to sacrifice an animal. Jesus' actions showed he considered a pure heart more important than ritual following of laws.
   4. The normal human tendency is to love our friends but hate our enemies.
   5. Every person has great value and is deeply cared for by God.

5. Ask the participants to share any other personal insights they gleaned from any of the passages. Then, summarize. Say:

   One of the things that Catholic Christianity has always emphasized is the fact that Jesus was connected to, and valued, the ordinary "stuff" in life. He himself was a part of the world: he ate, drank, and slept like you and I. He took time for the small ordinary things, and, for him, they had great meaning. Jesus presented them as things which could reveal God's presence. As Jesus' followers, we, too, look for meaning for God's presence in the things we can taste, touch, and do.

Activity: Looking Deeply at Our Lives

6. Ask the participants to gather around the display table where you have collected some mementos of your life. Lift the cloth covering the table, point out the mementos, and say:

   This table contains some pretty ordinary things. But they are really not so ordinary for me because of some deeper meanings they have. They remind me of some important times in my life. They help me to recall experiences, events, and relationships that have taught me about life and its purpose and have made me who I am. When I look at these things, I see in them much more than you do. These are symbols charged with meaning for me.

7. Proceed by telling a part of your life story using one or more of the mementos. Emphasize the experiences, events, or relationships that the mementos are associated with. Some may be one-time events (e.g., a vacation or prom); others may be associated with repeated events or traditions (e.g., Christmas celebration, a marriage).

8. Have the participants return to the small group tables. Pass out a piece of newsprint and a set of markers to each group. Ask them to think about mementos they would gather to tell the story of who they are. Read the following list, pausing between each item for marking. Add some other common events or experiences of your own. Say:

   As I mention each event or experience, draw a word or symbol that represents it on the newsprint:

   - a happy event
   - a time you cried
   - a great success
   - a surprise
   - a major decision you made
   - an important relationship
   - a broken friendship
   - an award you won

   Now take turns around the table. When it is your turn, point to any word or symbol and ask the person who wrote that item to first tell his or her name (and school, grade, etc.), and then explain its meaning. Keep taking turns until time is called.

9. Allow a few more minutes for discussion. Then summarize the activity and this part of the session. Say:

   If you actually had the mementos you drew or wrote about here with you, they would help you to recall more about what is important to you and what you hope for. Symbolic mementos of this kind can help you and others understand who you really are.

Break

(about 5 minutes)

Allow time for a brief stretch, drink of water, etc. Tell the participants to meet in the large meeting area near the television monitor after the break. During the break, make final preparations for the video segment you plan to present.

Part II: The Church Continues Jesus' Way of Seeing

(about 50 minutes)

Video Prelude

1. Briefly introduce and then play the video segment you have chosen depicting an area of Jesus' public ministry.

   Optional: Display a poster depicting one or more events of Jesus' ministry. Recreate the accompanying scripture passage and tell the story in your own words.

2. Point out the importance of the event, words, or actions depicted in the video. Ask the participants to name some tangible signs or "mementos" that can help to remind people through the ages of its significance (e.g., water/baptism, bread/meal stories, oil/healings). List on the board the ideas they come up with.

Jesus' Mementos

3. Ask the participants to sit in a circle. Place the items you have collected to represent Jesus' life, teachings, and ministry on the floor in the center of the circle. Say:

   > The first Christians took tangible signs of Jesus' life, teachings, and ministry to help succeeding generations remember and keep Jesus alive in their midst. Some items similar to those in the center of the circle helped them to remember. (Pick up the old coin.) For example, seeing an old coin like this may have helped the first Christians remember Jesus' story of the poor widow who donated her precious two coins to the Temple treasury, or Jesus' pulling a coin from the mouth of a fish to pay his share of the government tax, or even Jesus' overturning of the money changers tables in the Temple vestibule. How do these other items in the center of the circle help you to remember something about Jesus?

4. Call on one participant to choose an item, hold it, and tell how he or she associates a remembrance of Jesus with the item. Use the following examples to help:

Examples

- An old sandal is remindful of Jesus' traveling on the dusty roads of Galilee, of his feet-washing at the Last Supper.
- A cloth bandage is remindful of Jesus' raising of Lazaraus and the removal of his burial cloths.
- A loaf of bread is remindful of the many meals Jesus' shared with his followers.
- A small seed is remindful of the parable of the mustard seed.
- A crutch is remindful of Jesus' healings.
- A cross is remindful of the way that Jesus was crucified.

5. Call on other volunteers to repeat the process for the other mementos. Point out that the early Christians did not attempt this challenge on their own; rather, they were aided by the power of the Holy Spirit and the very words of Christ.

Scripture Investigation

6. Have the participants return to their table groups and open to page 10, "What the First Christians Experienced." Tell them to follow this format to investigate some of the significant events experienced by the early Christians: (1) select a person to read the passage aloud; (2) discuss and write the significant event or experience remembered in the passage; and (3) discuss and write tangible signs and symbolic actions that would help Christians from all ages recall and relive the event or experience.

   Take the participants through Acts 2:41-47 as an example. The significant events or experiences in the passage are baptism, communal life, breaking of the bread, prayers, and aid to the poor. Tangible signs and symbolic actions that help recall these experiences are water, church buildings or gathering places, bread, wine, codified prayers, agencies to help the poor, etc.

7. Allow time for the groups to work through each passage. Call on a volunteers to share the events and tangible signs they have come up for each passage. As the examples of signs are shared, star any on the list on the board that are similar. Add any that are new.

Answers

Acts 2:41-47. See above.

Acts 6:1-7. The significant event is the calling of leaders. Some tangible signs of this event are prayer and the laying on of hands.

Acts 8:14-17. The significant event is the reception of the Holy Spirit. A tangible sign to remember this event is the laying on of hands by the apostles.

Acts 10:44-48. The significant event is the initiation of Gentile members into the Christian community. Some tangible signs are water and prayer.

Ephesians 5:25-32. The significant experience is comparing the love of husbands and wives to that of the love Christ has for the church. The sign is marriage.

James 5:13-17. The significant experience is consolation when one experiences poor health. Some signs are the prayer and anointing of the sick person by the presbyter of the church.

1 John 1:5-10. The significant experience is the forgiveness of sins. The sign is the power given by Jesus to his apostles to forgive sins.

8. Go back through the list of tangible signs and symbolic actions. Point out that the church has given the name sacrament to seven of the significant events or experiences in the life of the early Christians. Call on volunteers to identify the sacrament described in each passage. Then, ask a good reader to read the definition of sacrament on page 12. Point out the three categories for the seven sacraments. In conclusion, say:

> Through these tangible signs and reminders—the sacraments—Jesus is truly alive for us. When we have the "eyes" to see more deeply, the symbols and actions of the seven sacraments have potential to make a significant difference in our lives, to move us in the direction of love and service away from sin and selfishness. In this course, we will be examining more closely the meanings of each of the seven sacraments.

Prayer Experience: Gifted with the Eyes of Faith

(about 15 minutes)

1. Play a recording of instrumental music and ask the participants to reverently enter the prayer space and sit around the centering cloth. Light the candle and place it near the bowl of holy water. After the group is quieted, call on the teen you have prepared to read the passage from John 9:1-11.

2. After the reading, say:

> Through the waters of baptism, you have entered a people whose eyes have been opened, who see life through the lens of Jesus. As a sign of our Christian identity, let us sign ourselves with the cross of Christ. When the bowl of holy water is passed to you, take a moment to remember a person in your life who has helped you to see life in a new way, someone whose optimism and visionary way of seeing life has affected you. Say something like, "for my uncle John who has been an example of patience," make the sign of the cross, and pass the bowl to the next person.

3. Begin the process with your own prayer of thanksgiving. Make the sign of the cross and pass the bowl to the person next to you. Remind the participants of the pass option.

4. When the bowl is back to you, close by saying:

You have been marked with the sign of Christ. You belong to him and have been gifted with the eyes of faith. May you walk always in the direction of the reign of God as the Spirit leads you. Amen.

Feedback and Conclusion

(about 10 minutes)

1. Gather again in the large meeting area. Tape three pieces of newsprint on different walls. Print one of the following words on each newsprint: insight, question, experience.
2. Tell the participants to think about what they gained from this session. Say:

   If you had one new insight, learned something new, or considered something you have never thought about before, stand at the area marked "insight." If this session raised new questions for you, about the sacraments, about Jesus, about your faith, about why you are in this course, stand at the area marked "question." If what you'll remember about this session is an experience you had, meeting someone new, doing an activity, discussing your faith with others, stand at the area marked "experience."

3. Ask for volunteers from each area to tell you about any insights, to ask a question, or to share a memorable experience. Hear from as many people as time allows.

Mentor Meeting Reminder

4. At this first session, it is important to clarify the teen-mentor meeting assignment. Remind the participants to bring their books to their meetings, to complete the teen-mentor meeting summary (page 14 of the Participant Book), and to have the page signed by their mentor and returned at the next group session.

Home Assignment

5. Tell the participants to bring to Session Two a baby photo of themselves with their name lightly printed on the back.
6. Dismiss the group on time. Tell them you will see them on the date of Session Two.

Sacraments of Initiation: Are You Ready to Take the Plunge?

Session Two

Objectives

The purpose of this session is to help the participants:

- view the sacraments of initiation as a ritual process to mark conversion and the acceptance of the Christian way of life;
- examine some of the ways the processes of initiation are experienced in the church today;
- experience the symbolic language of Christian initiation.

Overview

"Who am I?" and "Who am I becoming?" are perennial questions during adolescence, but they also continue to follow us through other stages of life. In order to know what to do, we must know something of who we are—specifically, something of our roots and of the groups to which we belong. In learning who we are, we discover several ways to join in. This journey of belonging is not done alone, but with others who are also in the process of becoming. Christian initiation, as celebrated in baptism, confirmation, and eucharist, ritually names the reality of our becoming. These signposts publicly mark the beginning of our journey in, with, and to Christ. Although baptism, confirmation, and eucharist are distinct sacraments, each with its own theology, they must also be seen as part of a common movement that leads people into full membership in Christ's body, the church. This session emphasizes the theological unity of the sacraments of initiation, while affirming that the initiation of adults and the issues they face in conversion are different from those of children and youth. Eucharist, the central sacrament of the church, is the focus of Sessions Three and Four.

Mentor Component

Preview Teen-Mentor Meeting 2. Note the three activity suggestions and provide information about dates, times, and places for each. Also, you may consider assigning teen-and-mentor pairs as prayer partners with adult catechumens or parents of infant initiates as part of an ongoing activity to last the duration of the course.

Session Outline

Opening Activity: What's My Line? (about 20 minutes)

Part I: On the Road to Find Out . . . Who I Am (about 50 minutes)

Organized Nonsense and Break (about 15 minutes)

Part II: Celebrating the Roadposts Along the Way (about 35 minutes)

Prayer Experience: Walking Through the Rituals of Initiation (about 20 minutes)

Feedback and Conclusion (about 10 minutes)

Supplies

For this session you will need:

- pencils or pens
- extra copies of the Participant Book for guests
- baby photo of each participant
- extra display table
- small adhesive notes
- copies of Resource 2, "Class Yearbook Tally Sheet" (one for each small group)
- large sheets of paper
- thick marker
- tape
- (optional) acetate copy of Resource 3, "Group Initiation Chart"
- (optional) acetate copy of Resource 4, "Church Initiation Chart"
- (optional) overhead projector and screen
- copy of Resource 5, "Christian Initiation Speaker Preparation Sheet"
- (optional) video on the adult Christian catechumenate process; e.g., *RCIA: Invitation to Life* (Paulist Press) or *This Is the Night* (Liturgy Training Publications)
- small cloth ball (or any easily catchable ball)
- *Lion King* video
- (optional) *Godparent Gussie* (Teleketics) video
- VCR and monitor

- six copies of Resource 6, "Walking through the Rituals of Initiation"
- three display tables
- tablecloths or linens for each table
- large clay pot or bowl with holy water
- a small bowl
- a flask of oil
- a small towel
- a basket with bread, partially sliced
- an enthroned bible
- a book of Rites for the sacraments
- a recording of instrumental music or flowing water sounds
- a recording of "Circle of Life" from the *Lion King* soundtrack
- an Easter candle

Special Preparations

1. Prepare signs naming various groups that teens belong to (see Part I, No. 1).
2. Arrange for an adult who has involvement in the parish Christian initiation program (a new initiate, a sponsor, a core team member) to address the teens about his or her experience in the various stages of initiation. Provide the speaker with Resource 5, "Christian Initiation Speaker Preparation Sheet."
3. Cue the *Lion King* video to the opening scene of Simba's dedication.
4. See the optional note in Part I, No. 5 for suggestions involving other guest presenters.
5. Prepare six teens as readers for the Prayer Experience. Have them review their parts from Resource 6.

Settings

You will need the following areas for this session:

1. A large area where the participants can gather in a relaxed and comfortable atmosphere for large-group discussions. The room should have an open space from which the participants can easily view a chalkboard. An extra display table should be set up so that the participants can easily gather around it.
2. An area where teens can gather around circular tables in groups of six to eight.
3. An area for the Prayer Experience. The floor of the church sanctuary often works well. If this area is impossible to use, arrange the large-group area into a comfortable setting for prayer. Three display tables should be placed in the center of the space: one with a large bowl of holy water, one with a flask of oil, one with a basket of bread. Each display should be covered with a cloth or linen as the participants enter the prayer space. The large Easter candle should be positioned near the three tables.

Opening Activity: What's My Line?

(about 20 minutes)

Welcome/Check-in

1. As the participants arrive, greet each by name and collect their baby photos. Make sure their names are lightly printed on the backs. Have them check in with their group moderators and show the summary page and mentor's verification signature for Teen-Mentor Meeting 1. While this is taking place, arrange the baby photos on the display table. Number the photos using small adhesive notes.
2. When the display table is ready, ask the participants to turn to page 16 in the Participant Book, "Class Yearbook" and read the directions. Allow them to assemble around the display table and work individually to fill in the spaces with the corresponding numbers.
3. After about five minutes, tell the groups to return to their tables. Designate a recorder at each table and have him or her tally the votes for each category on Resource 2, "Class Yearbook Tally Sheet." Then, call on each recorder to come to the board one at a time and add to the running total (erase old totals, write new ones) of votes for the photo numbers and categories. Make sure everyone can view the board as the adding is taking place. The board should look like this (for example):

Photo Number	1	2	3	4	5	6	7	8	9	10
Peacemaker		3	1		7		2	1		1
President		4		6	1	1	2			1
Rock Star					8	2		1	3	4

4. After the tallying is complete, ask each person to introduce himself or herself in the following or similar format: "My name is John. I'm number 7 and the majority of you think that I will be a hair stylist." Or, simply announce the names and winners for each category.
5. Summarize the opening activity by reading the opening text on page 15.

Part I: On the Road to Find Out . . .Who I Am

(about 50 minutes)

1. Designate sections of the large meeting area with posted signs listing four groups that teens belong to; e.g., teams, scouts, band, school government, youth group. Include groups common to the teens that you work with. Also include a fifth category called "other." Say:

Please sit near the sign describing the group that has had the most influence on your becoming who you are. If you choose the "other" section, be prepared to tell the name or what kind of group you are referring to.

Panel Discussion

2. When everyone is seated near a sign, ask each formed group to select its "least shy" member to be on a panel (see Appendix, page 121). Assemble the panel in the front of the group. Then dialogue with them about why they have named the group they have chosen as having the most influence on them. Use the following questions. Add more of your own.

Questions

- When were you a member of the group?
- What is the name of the group?
- Why did you want to be a member of the group?
- What did you have to do to become a member?
- What did you have to do while you were a member?
- How did the group have an influence on you?
- What were the rewards of being a member?

After a few minutes of discussion you may wish to select a second group of panelists (one from each category, or all those from the "other" category).

3. At the conclusion of the panel discussion, say:

Life is often described as a journey, with each choice we make creating a new road on a "life map." The influence of the groups you belong to—not just the one's we have discussed, but also family and friends—reminds us that we do not travel alone. Much of the task of living is taken up with belonging: to family, to peer groups, to organizations, to schools, to teams, to occupations, to our nation, to the church. In the next exercise we are going to take a closer look at some of the dynamics associated with becoming members of a group.

Grouping/Exercise

4. Use the existing groups seated near the signs to help you form five table groups of equal size. When everyone is seated, assign each group one of the following group identities: medical doctors, professional athletes, military officers, American citizens, or college fraternity/sorority members. Have them write their group identity at the top of the first chart on page 17. Then, say:

Choose one person in each group to be an "inquirer" and ask question number one from "Inquirer's Questions" aloud. Then go around the group with each person sharing one personal quality needed to be a member. As each person shares, write the personal qualities mentioned on your chart. Next, ask question two. Go around the group again and write down ideas in column two. Continue the same process for questions three and four.

5. Allow about fifteen minutes for the groups to complete the first chart. Call on a volunteer from each group to share some of the responses for each category. Summarize their responses on the board. Refer to Resource 3 for some more ideas.

   Optional: Make an acetate copy of Resource 3 and uncover each category one-by-one on an overhead projector and screen as the participants share their reports.

6. Say:

   In the all the various interpersonal relationships we have in life, a formal or informal initiation process is likely to be in place to welcome new members. This is true in our membership in friendship and peer groups, in workplaces, in neighborhoods, and even in families. Likewise, the church—as a living collection of people—has processes to initiate new members. Imagine you were asked the questions on page 17 by a person wanting to join the Catholic church. How would you answer?

7. Allow a few minutes for quiet thinking. Then work together with all the participants to fill in the chart on page 18 of the Participant Book. Draw as much information as possible from the participants. Write the key phrases on the board and ask the participants to write them in their books as you go along. Resource 4 provides a key with information to add to the ideas covered by the participants.

   Optional: Make an acetate copy of Resource 4 and uncover each category one-by-one on an overhead projector and screen as the participants share their reports.

8. Ask the participants by show of hands how many of them underwent an initiation process for entering the Catholic church as described on the chart. (Likely very few will raise their hands.) Explain that the process that you have laid out is a Christian initiation process for adults. Ask how many have heard of the initials **RCIA** (write on the board)? Call on a volunteer to tell you what the initials stand for (Rite of Christian Initiation of Adults). Say:

   The RCIA is the church's formal process of initiation for adults who have never been baptized. It is also called the **catechumenate** (write), a word that means **"period of instruction"** (write). The adult who seeks membership in the church is called a catechumen. This person has been led by his or her own "life map" into a journey of conversion leading to full membership in the Catholic community. The formal initiation usually happens at the Easter vigil where he or she receives the sacraments of initiation: baptism, confirmation and eucharist.

Guest Speaker Presentation

9. Introduce the guest speaker you have invited to address the group on his or her participation in the parish's Christian initiation process. Allow ten minutes for the presentation and at least five minutes for the participants to ask questions.

   Optional: In lieu of the guest speaker, play all or part of a video that introduces the **RCIA** process; for example, *RCIA: An Invitation to New Life* (Paulist Press) or *This Is the Night* (Liturgy Training Publications).

Organized Nonsense and Break

(about 15 minutes)

Energizer

1. Divide the group in half and tell them to stand and face each other in parallel lines. Produce a cloth-type ball. Say:

> When you are thrown the ball you will be given five seconds to name a person in the line across from you and something you have in common with him or her. It can be as simple as "Kevin. We both have brown hair." Or, "Abby. We both live on Pearl Street." After you have named and shared, throw the ball to someone else in the line across from you. You can only name a person one time.

Play the game until everyone has had a chance to talk.

Break

2. Allow a brief time for a break before continuing. Tell the participants to assemble after the break near the television monitor with their books and pencils.

Part II: Celebrating the Roadposts Along the Way

(about 35 minutes)

1. Introduce *The Lion King* video segment (cued to opening scene of Simba's dedication). Tell the participants to watch it, keeping in mind what they learned about the initiation process from their responses to the inquirers' questions on page 17.
2. After playing the video, ask the participants to move to "alone" spots with a partner and discuss the questions on page 18 of the Participant Book. Allow five to ten minutes for discussion. Then call everyone near the board and draw from the participants the following answers to each question.

   Questions and Answers
   - What ceremony marked Simba's membership in the community? (The pouring of and marking with sand.)
   - What qualities did baby Simba have that indicated his readiness to take on the way of life of the king? (None. He was a baby.)
   - What kind of apprenticeship process did Simba go through prior to the ceremony? (The process came after the ceremony, not before.)
   - How did Simba grow into the role of king? (He gradually learned what was expected of a king. He learned about these expectations from his parents, Nala, and others in the community.)

- Why do you think Simba was dedicated king as a young cub, rather than when he was old enough to accept the role for himself. (His parents, family, and community wanted to share the expectations they had for his life from the very beginning.)
- How is this scene from *The Lion King* reminiscent of Christian initiation? (It is reminiscent of the baptism of infants. Infants are not able to indicate their willingness or readiness to be Christians. They are not capable of understanding any form of an apprenticeship or initiation process. Rather, it is their parents, family, and church community that accept the faith for them. Parents and other adult members do this for infants because this is an important part of the identity they seek for their children and they believe that being part of the Christian community is what their children are called to be.)

3. Write the names of the two processes of Christian initiation on the board: **Rite of Christian Initiation of Adults** and **Rite of Baptism of Children**. Say:

The Christian initiation processes for adults and children have basically the same elements, but in reverse order. Adult initiation in an RCIA process is marked by the experiences of initial conversion, followed by a journey of Christian apprenticeship, and culminating in the reception of the sacraments of baptism, confirmation, and eucharist. The Rite of Baptism for Children outlines a process in which baptism comes first, followed by a period where the child learns and grows in his or her faith, culminating in a time when he or she makes a personal decision to accept faith. You may be wondering why the church has two initiation processes. Why not initiate only adults or only children? To understand that part of the story we need to take a brief look at history.

4. Summarize the material on pages 19-20, "Walking Back to the Beginning," or have the participants silently read it on their own.
   Optional: Play the video *Godparent Gussie* (Teleketics), covering the historical development of the sacraments of initiation.

Public Interview

5. Use the public interview technique (see Appendix, page 121) to review the historical development of Christian initiation and address some of the contemporary issues surrounding infant baptism. Ask two or three of the following questions (and some of your own) of each participant you call to be interviewed.

Sample Questions

- Who was the main presider at baptisms prior to 313? (The bishop.)
- What happened in 313 to change the way Christians were initiated? (Christianity was legalized; many sought to go "public" with their faith.)
- Were you baptized as an infant? How do you feel about that?
- Who are your godparents? What have you learned about the Christian faith from them?

- If you were a parent, would you have your infant baptized or would you wait until the child could make his or her own choice about accepting the Christian faith? Why?
- What do you remember about your preparation for first eucharist? Were there any requirements you had to fulfill?
- Tell about the day you received first eucharist. Who was there? How did you celebrate?
- At what age will (did) you receive confirmation? How do you understand the meaning of confirmation?
- Why do some people think it important that the sacraments be celebrated in one movement: baptism, confirmation, eucharist?
- Reordering leads the sacraments to take on separate meanings of their own apart from the initiation process. What do you think about this?

Call on as many participants as time allows. Include some adults in the interview process.

Optional: Invite a couple who have recently had a child baptized (along with the child) to tell why they chose baptism. Then invite all the participants to sign the child's forehead with the sign of the cross. Or, ask one or two teenagers who have been recently confirmed to talk about the experience and how they are trying to live as committed disciples.

Prayer Experience:
Walking Through the Rituals of Initiation

(about 20 minutes)

1. Begin the recording of instrumental music or sounds of flowing water and light the Easter candle. Invite the participants to enter the area you have reserved for prayer and stand around the first table. Uncover the cloth revealing the large bowl of water. Call on Reader 1 to read his or her part from Resource 6, "Walking Through the Rituals of Initiation." After the reading, say:

   Come forward to the holy water, and bless yourself in the name of the Father and of the Son and of the Holy Spirit. Remain around the table until everyone has blessed themselves.

   After everyone has been blessed, call on the second reader to read his or her part.

2. Direct the group to the second table. Uncover the cloth to reveal the flask of oil. Ask the third reader to proceed. Next, pour the oil into a small bowl. Make a sign of the cross on the hands of the person on one side of you. Pass the bowl and a cloth for wiping and direct the person to sign the hands of the next person. Continue until everyone has been signed. Then call on the fourth reader to read his or her part.

3. Move with the group to the third table. Uncover the cloth to reveal the basket of bread. Ask the fifth reader to begin. Break off a chunk of bread, and pass the loaf to a person next to you. Tell the participants to wait until everyone has a slice before eating. Then ask the sixth reader to read his or her part.
4. Direct the participants to have a seat on the floor. (Or, if the mood is right, to stand in a circle and hold hands.) Begin playing "The Circle of Life" from *The Lion King* track. Conclude by reciting together an Our Father.

Feedback and Conclusion

(about 10 minutes)

Journal Activity

1. Ask the participants to meet again at their tables. Go over the directions for the Journal Activity on page 21 and allow about five minutes for the participants to begin writing. Remind them to finish the Journal Activity prior to meeting with their mentor.

Mentor Meeting Reminder

2. Preview Teen-Mentor Meeting 2 on pages 22-23 in the Participant Book. Have the participants record in the Mentor Memo space any specific messages to the mentors (e.g., the times and places of the meetings mentioned in the activity suggestions). Remind them to take their books to the meeting and to complete the required summary by the time that it is due.
3. Dismiss the participants on time. Tell them you will see them on <u>the date of Session Three</u>.

Session Three

Eucharist, Part I: You Really Are What You Eat

Objectives

The purpose of this session is to help the participants:

- connect with the universal experience of sharing bread as a sign of life and unity;
- understand the significance of meal-sharing in Jesus' ministry and in the early church's eucharistic practice;
- discover and explore the rhythm of the eucharistic liturgy.

Overview

The journey of conversion reaches its apex at eucharist. This is the moment when we can proclaim publicly, "Yes, I believe that I am loved by God. Yes, I believe that I am part of God's saving activity. Yes, I promise to live my life with others in ways that will build God's reign of love, peace, justice, and unity." These affirmations are proclaimed publicly in the breaking and eating of bread, the pouring and drinking of wine. In these sacred actions, Jesus' life is truly one with ours. In this sense, we really are what we eat. This session helps the participants name some of the experiences associated with meal-sharing, including occasions of welcoming, celebrating, belonging, and caring. The participants compare some of the actions of contemporary meals with those of Jesus' ministry and of eucharist. In prayer, the participants remember the specific needs of others in the world who share the common need of physical and spiritual nourishment.

Mentor Component

Preview Teen-Mentor Meeting 3. Activity Suggestion 3 calls for the teens and mentors to speak with a member of a parish liturgy planning team as a way to involve themselves in a liturgical ministry. Contact the person responsible and inform him or her of this suggestion. Plan for the teens to note their person's phone number in the Mentor Memo panel.

Session Three

Session Outline

Opening Activity: Breads of Life (about 20 minutes)

Part I: Meals Are More than Just Three Squares a Day (about 50 minutes)

Break (about 5 minutes)

Part II: Eucharist: A Life-Giving Meal for All Time (about 40 minutes)

Prayer Experience: Sharing Our Stories With Others (about 15 minutes)

Feedback and Conclusion (about 20 minutes)

Supplies

For this session you will need:

- pencils or pens
- extra copies of the Participant Book
- an assortment of various types of breads (e.g., tortillas, sandwich bread, dinner rolls, breadsticks, baby biscuits, sweet bread, matzo, etc.)
- bibles
- (optional) acetate copy of Resource 7, "Jesus' Meal Ministry"
- (optional) overhead projector and screen
- nine copies of Resource 8, "Bread of Life"
- a news reporter's interview props (a notepad and pencil or a "microphone")
- candle
- recording of "Lord, To Whom Shall We Go?" by Tom Conry (New Dawn Music, Portland, OR) or any familiar eucharistic song
- tape or CD player
- scrap paper

Special Preparations

1. Choose and prepare nine participants for roles in a skit "Bread of Life" (Part II, No. 1). Give each a copy of Resource 8. For the role of Jesus choose an adult or teen you feel will do an exceptionally good job.
2. Choose and prepare a teen to read Luke 24:13-35 for the Prayer Experience.
3. (optional) Choose two participants to mime the actions of the two disciples as the story of Emmaus is read during the Prayer Experience.
4. (optional) Arrange for one or two members of the liturgy committee to speak to the group about ways that teens can become more involved in liturgy and liturgy planning at your parish (see Feedback and Conclusion, No. 3).

Settings

You will need the following areas for this session:

1. A large area where the participants can gather in a relaxed and comfortable atmosphere for large-group discussions. The room should have an open space from which the participants can easily view a chalkboard or easel. Prepare a display table with the various types of bread and with enough room on each side so that the participants can gather around.
2. An area where teens can gather around circular tables in groups of six to eight.
3. "Alone" spots—places where the participants can be at least six feet away from everyone else.
4. An area for the Prayer Experience. This should be handled in the large meeting area near the bread display table. If possible, provide cushions or floor pillows for the participants to sit on during this time.

Opening Activity: Breads of Life

(about 20 minutes)

Welcome

1. Greet the participants as they arrive and ask them to gather in the large meeting area. When all are present, introduce the session theme by reading the opening story on page 25 of the Participant Book. Then ask everyone to stand around the display table with the breads. Say:

> The narrator of the story described a scene where people of all kinds were brought together on a busy street corner, attracted in some way to the warmth and aroma of bread emanating from the bake shop. Bread has been called the "staff of life" because in most cultures it is the basic source of nourishment. Hardly a meal goes by in which bread in one form or another is not served. I am going to describe a meal scene and call on a volunteer to name the kind of bread that might be served, as well as some of the mood, atmosphere, and words that could be a part of that meal. When the person is through with the description, others may add more details and information about the scene.

2. Present the following scenes one at a time. Choose volunteers to name the kind of bread that may be served and to describe the meal setting, who might be there, some of the topics of conversation, and the mood of the occasion. Allow others to comment before moving on to the next scene.

Scenes

- A sister in a Tijuana orphanage prepares the day's main meal for the forty children who live at the home. (tortilla)
- During the football game, friends gather near a television set to watch. (pizza)

- A girl invites a new student to eat with her on the school lunch bench. (sandwich bread)
- Friends, family, bride and groom gather at the banquet hall after the wedding. (rolls)
- The baby's first teeth are in and he can now sit in a high chair near the family table. (baby biscuits)
- A Jewish family celebrates the Passover. (matzo)
- A dad is brought a special birthday breakfast in bed. (waffles, French toast, pancakes)

3. When seated, have the participants turn to page 25. Point out the space for writing at the bottom of the page. Ask them to finish the sentence, "Meals are about. . . ." with as many examples as they can think of. Tell them to use the previous examples for clues. Allow about three minutes for writing. Then call on volunteers to share their responses. Record on the board. If not mentioned, add the following to the list:
    - **sustenance**
    - **celebration**
    - **welcoming new people into the group**
    - **expressing honor**
    - **sharing gratitude for a job well done, a life well lived**
    - **companionship**
    - **looking forward to the future**
    - **religious and family significance**
4. Tell the participants to write in their books on page 25 the additional suggestions from the board.

Part I: Meals Are More than Just Three Squares a Day

(about 50 minutes)

1. Remain with the group in the large meeting area. Then present a talk based on the following story. Either read the story or tell it in your own words.

Alex Remembers Story

2. It was December 20. First semester finals had come to an end and Alex Weaver was ready to go home for Christmas. Well, not exactly home, but the word did seem more comfortable to him than it ever had before. Alex really did consider the Harris's house his holiday home since he had spent the past three Christmases there. For a moment, he thought about the next Christmas and where he would be. This was his last year of college and he and his friend Mark would probably go their separate ways after graduation. He dismissed the thoughts . . . this was a time for appreciating what he had.

Mark slept as usual on the three-hour bus ride. Alex sat and stared out the window. He thought of his friendship with Mark and his first Christmas at the Harris's. Alex and Mark had become instant friends during the first days of their freshman year, drawn together as members of the scout football team. Day after day at practice, Alex and Mark took a pounding from the older players. It seemed that misery did love company!

But Alex dreaded the holidays as they approached. The others in the dorm would find out that he had no place to go. As a kid he had grown up in five different foster homes and really had not bothered to keep much contact with any of them. Alex had never met his father; the last he heard his mother was living somewhere in California.

Alex told Mark only that, "I'm just going to hang around here during Christmas."

Mark didn't ask any questions. Rather, he said, "I hope you come home with me for Christmas." Alex was nervous about accepting the invitation and intruding on a family Christmas celebration, but after a little thought, he figured it would definitely be better than spending the holidays alone. He used the next couple of days to get ready, buying a gift for Mark and another one for Mark's parents.

"Alex, welcome!" Mark's mom greeted him at the door. "We are glad you are going to be with us at Christmas. Please make yourself at home."

Alex had been in so many different homes in his life he could always tell how much he was inconveniencing a family by his presence. Yet from the moment he first came to the Harris's, he felt genuinely welcomed.

The next night, Christmas Eve, was even more heartening. Before they came to the dinner table, the family gathered in the living room around the tree. Alex could tell that something special was about to happen. It seemed that there was a family tradition that went like this: at the Thanksgiving dinner, everyone had chosen a name of another family member. During the days before Christmas each person prayed for his or her partner. On Christmas Eve, finally, each person's "secret Santa" was revealed. The best part of the tradition was that each person wrote a letter and gave a present to their chosen person. All the letters were read aloud.

There was silence while each letter was read. The letters said something unique about the person and mentioned how they were an important part of the family. Lots of love and memories went into each letter. Many of the letters expressed sorrow for some wrong one family member had done to another. After Mark read an apology to his younger sister Laura for being angry over the way she redesigned his old bedroom, the two laughed and hugged right in front of everyone else. If fact, all of these people expressed things about others that Alex had barely thought of, much less ever considered sharing publicly. Twelve letters were read in all. It seemed the occasion was over. But then Mark stood up again. He read a second letter and this one was about Alex! It talked about how Alex had helped him make a good transition to college. Alex remembered one line in particular: "Coming from a family of all girls, you've really been a brother to me." Then Mark's parents gave Alex a present. He opened it to find a wool blanket, perfect for the winter months they were to face back in the dorm. Alex had been happy just to observe this family tradition. Now he found he was himself a participant!

Soon everyone moved to the dining room table. A special blessing prayer was said and the dinner was served. Mark's older sister brought a sweet potato casserole that she was eager to share. His brother-in-law had some homemade bread (a new hobby). Mark's mom engineered the rest of the meal. As the family ate, they continued to reminisce and share stories. Alex felt comfortable enough to add some recent stories about college life. Minutes turned to hours. The dishes were cleared, dessert came and went, but everyone stayed around the table talking.

When everyone finally got up to leave, Alex felt disappointed. Couldn't the good feeling last a little longer? Best wishes and farewells were exchanged since not everyone would be back again the next day for Christmas. Two of Mark's sisters were planning to serve dinner at a homeless shelter. Mark's older sister and husband were off to the in-laws, and Mark's parents were going to visit his grandma who was bed-bound in a nursing home.

Each of the next two Christmas's were very much the same. Now, it would likely be his last holiday visit with the Harris's. Looking out the bus window, Alex was sad at the thought. But he would always be grateful for these special holidays when he received a gift that he believed would remain with him forever.

Journal Activity

3. After the story, ask the participants to move to an alone spot with their books and a pencil. Instruct them to write their responses to each question on pages 26-27, "Meals to Remember." Allow about ten minutes for writing.

Grouping/Discussion

4. Use one of the grouping suggestions (see Appendix, pages 122-124) to form groups of six to eight participants each and meet at tables. Ask the participants to go around the table one at a time and share any one response to the "Alex" entries. After everyone has shared, ask them to repeat the process and share any one of the responses to the "You" entries.

Scripture Exercise

5. Call on runners to pick up bibles (one for each person) for their tables. Turn to "Jesus Meal Ministry" on pages 28-29. Read aloud the first passage, the feeding of the five thousand (Mk 6:34-44), as the participants read along. Then ask volunteers to suggest adjectives for the three columns on the chart. Write the responses on the board, for example:

before the Meal?	during the Meal with Jesus?	after the Meal?
lonely, scared, cold	surprised, content, loved	generous, compelled to act, energized

6. Ask the groups to work together to finish filling in the chart. Say:

Choose one person to read a scripture passage aloud as everyone follows along. Then go around the group suggesting adjectives that describe the feelings of the meal guests at each of the listed times.

Allow about fifteen minutes for reading and discussion. Then call on volunteers to summarize their group's responses for each passage. Record the adjectives on the board, forming a chart as on pages 28-29 in the Participant Book.

Optional: Make an acetate copy of Resource 7, "Jesus' Meal Ministry" and record the answers as the participants share. Project the chart using an overhead projector and screen.

Public Interviews

7. Ask the participants to meet in the large meeting area near the board. Then ask for a volunteer who would be willing to dialogue with you in front of the group. Give this person a chair and ask him or her to face the others. Point to the second set of adjectives on the chart for Zacchaeus. Say:

> I would like you to take the role of Zacchaeus and explain to us why you felt the way you did before, during, and after your meal with Jesus. Why did you feel alienated (use adjectives the participants have suggested) when Jesus entered your village? (Allow the volunteer to answer.) Why were you surprised when Jesus came to eat with you? (Pause.) Why do you now feel committed to follow Jesus? (Pause.)

Call on other volunteers to take the roles of Levi, someone in the crowd of five thousand, the sinful woman, and Martha or Mary. Ask them "why" questions based on the adjectives listed for each column on the board. Choose as many volunteers as you have time for.

8. As a way of concluding the scripture exercise, say:

> Jesus used the occasion of a meal to evoke positive change in a person's life. This model holds truth for us today as well, as witnessed in Alex's story and the remembrances of your own special meals. After the break we will examine how the eucharist likewise includes meal-sharing rituals we are familiar with and is in itself life-giving.

Break

(about 5 minutes)

Allow time for a brief stretch, drink of water, etc. Tell the participants to meet in the large meeting area after the break. Have the actors you have chosen for the "Bread of Life" skit meet for last minute preparations.

Part II: Eucharist: A Life-Giving Meal for All Time

(about 40 minutes)

Bread of Life Skit

1. Ask all the participants (actors except for Jesus, and non-actors) to sit in the open space to simulate as closely as possible a marketplace atmosphere. Tell them that

Jesus will walk in on this scene. Cue the narrator to begin from the script on Resource 8.

2. After the skit is complete, reverse the public interview format by taking the role of a news reporter and interviewing a greater number of the people in the crowd. Some sample questions are given below.

Questions

- Excuse me, madam (sir)? Did you just hear the sermon of that prophet from Nazareth? What do you think he was trying to say?
- Were you present on that hillside yesterday? How do you explain what happened there?
- Have you heard the report of the things that happened on the lake last night? They claim he walked across the water. How do you explain that?
- What do you think that he meant when he said that those who believe in him will "eat his flesh and drink his blood"?
- After hearing all of this, do you still consider yourself one of his followers?

3. Continue. Say:

Hearing the words of Jesus in the "Bread of Life" skit is easier for us twenty centuries after the words were first spoken. We understand now that Jesus was preparing his disciples to move from experiencing Jesus' presence and care for them in the many meals they had shared to an understanding of the mystery of his ongoing presence in the meal known that would be known as the Lord's Supper, or eucharist. The apostles did not understand Jesus' words about eating his flesh and drinking his blood. But most stayed with him anyway. Not until after the Last Supper did they begin to see what he meant, and not until after his resurrection did they really understand.

4. Take the participants through the Last Supper account from Luke 22:14-20 to explain what a Jew would have understood by the following boldfaced words or phrases (write them on the board). As you go through the explanation from the notes below, ask the participants to underline the corresponding word or phrase in the scripture text reprinted on page 30 of the Participant Book.

Notes

5. **Gave thanks.** Jesus would have recited the *berekah*, the great prayer of the Jewish people, a thanksgiving to God for all of the gifts God had given them. The word "eucharist" itself means "thanksgiving."

Broke the bread. Breaking bread was a symbol of love and friendship to the Jews. To break bread with someone was to show that you loved them like a member of your own family.

Body. This was not a biological term to the Jews, but a personal term. People were their bodies. When Jesus said, "This is my body" he meant: "This is me, my person."

Blood. Blood to the Jew meant life. It had much the same sense to them that the word "heart" has to us today. Think of the common phrase, "I love you with all my heart." In Jesus' time, it would have made sense for a person to say, "I love you with all my blood."

New Covenant. The Jews had a covenant with Yahweh that held that Yahweh would be their God and offer his protection and they would be his people and obey his laws. In this passage, Jesus is making a new covenant: God will love us as a parent loves a child and we will love and serve God as sons and daughters.

Blood which will be shed for you. Solemn agreements were sealed in blood; the blood of a lamb was sprinkled on both parties of the agreement as a sign that they were entrusting their lives to one another. Jesus offers his blood to seal the new contract between God and us. (Remind the participants of the scene in Tom Sawyer when Tom and Huck seal an agreement with their blood.)

This Passover. Passover to the Jews meant much the same as Fourth of July means to us. It was an occasion to celebrate freedom. Had Jesus been speaking to people today, he might have said, "This is a new Fourth of July." What would that mean? (Take comments from volunteers.)

Do this in memory of me. The Jews of Jesus' time believed that after death a person stayed alive in the nether world as long as someone on earth remembered them. That's why they recited the names of their ancestors as part of their religious feasts (Point out the genealogy of Jesus in Luke 3:23-38.) Jesus is asking his disciples to repeat this holy meal as a way of keeping him alive in the world after his death. Whenever we gather to "do this," Jesus promises to be present in our midst.

5. Have the participants move back to their tables and work individually to look up and read the scripture passages listed on page 31, "The Lord's Supper in the Early Church," and write a short essay telling about the important elements in the early church's celebration of eucharist. Allow a few minutes for everyone to finish. Then ask the participants to go around the table sharing what they wrote. Call on volunteers from each table to offer summaries of the key points. List them on the board. Possible responses are listed below:
    - **breaking of bread**
    - **entire community is welcome**
    - **held every day in homes; special mention of "the first day of the week"**
    - **participants must be cleansed before partaking**
    - **prayers of thanksgiving offered**
    - **those who ate bread and drank cup become one with Jesus and the community**
6. Next, read or summarize the text under the heading "The Eucharist Continues" on page 32. Write on the board the significant actions of eucharist: **gather, forgive, listen, share,** and **serve**. Ask the participants to share with their table groups how each action is present (1) in the "Alex Remembers" story, (2) in the Last Supper, and (3) at eucharist today. Allow a few minutes for discussion. Then call on a representative from each group to share the responses.

Prayer Experience:
Sharing Our Stories With Others

(about 15 minutes)

1. Prepare the prayer space. Move the display table with breads to the center of the room. Place a lighted candle in a corner of the table. Ask the participants to sit in a prayerful mood near the display table. Dim the lights and begin playing the recording of the eucharistic song you have selected.

The Emmaus Story

2. Call on the reader you have prepared to read the gospel story of Jesus' appearance on the road to Emmaus, Luke 24:13-35.

   Optional: Have two participants mime the parts of the two disciples as the story is read aloud. Jesus is represented only by their movements and facial expressions.
3. After the reading, share a homiletic reflection by dialoguing with participants. Ask several questions, including some of the sample questions listed below.

   Sample Questions

   - How was Jesus' presence different after his resurrection than before? How was it the same?
   - What does it take to convince you that Jesus is alive today?
   - What was the significance of the "breaking of the bread" in the story?
   - What does this gospel passage teach us about eucharist?
4. Ask the participants to stand and gather around the table. Say:

   Take a moment to think about a person you know who needs some type of nourishment (physical, emotional, spiritual). Or, think about person who provides these forms of nourishment for you. When you have this person in mind, take a piece of any of the bread as a sign of Jesus' presence among us. Then we will take turns offering prayers; for example, "For my friend who is really experiencing some hard times at home, we pray." We will respond, "Lord, hear our prayer."
5. Begin by breaking bread and offering your own prayer. Continue until everyone has taken a piece of bread. Then, offer a prayer in these or similar words:

   Jesus, you promised that you will be present whenever we gather and break bread in your name. Help us to be open to the life-giving power of the eucharist. Help us to be a welcoming people, willing to share your life with others. Thank you for inviting us to your table of life and for being with us now and forever. We pray in your name. Amen.
6. Eat your piece of bread and direct the others to do the same. If you wish, play again the recording of the eucharistic song.

Feedback and Conclusion

(about 20 minutes)

Attendance/Mentor Verification

1. Ask the groups to report to tables with their group moderators who will take attendance and check their summaries and mentor signatures from Teen-Mentor Meeting 2.

2. Pass out a stack of scrap paper to each table. Have them complete in writing the sentence **What I don't understand about eucharist is . . .** (write on board). Tell them they can complete the sentence with several statements. Ask them to go around the group sharing their responses. Allow a few minutes. Then poll each group on the most commonly mentioned statements.

3. Next, ask each person to complete the sentence **The best Mass I ever attended was . . .** (write). Then tell them to go around the table and share why this Mass was special. Ask each table to choose one person to briefly share his or her story with all.

4. Third, have the participants finish the sentence **If I were responsible for Sunday Masses at my parish I would . . .** (write). Ask them to go around the table and share. After the discussion, briefly tell them about some of the opportunities available at your parish for teens to participate in special ways in liturgy ("the work of the people") as musicians, eucharistic ministers, lectors, greeters, planners, and the like.

   Optional: Arrange for one or two representatives of the parish liturgy committee to come to the end of this session and tell the teens about some of the ways they might become more involved in the liturgy.

5. Collect all the papers. Plan to address at the next session some of the items that the teens said they did not understand. Also, invite them to write their questions in the "Mentor Memo" panel on page 33 and refer the questions to their mentors.

Mentor Meeting Reminder

6. Preview Teen-Mentor Meeting 3 on pages 33-34 in the Participant Book. Have the participants record any other specific messages to the mentors (e.g., the time and place of the video showing) in the Mentor Memo space. Remind them to take their books to the meeting and to complete the required summaries by the time that they are due.

Assignment

7. For Session Four, ask each participant to bring in a new toy that will be given to a young child. Remind the participants of the date of the next session. Dismiss them on time.

Eucharist, Part II: Don't Just Stand There

Session Four

Objectives

The purpose of this session is to help the participants

- understand the experience of presence to others in relation to the Catholic understanding of the real presence of Jesus at eucharist;
- explore the notion of sacrifice in relation to Jesus and eucharist;
- discover ways they can share Jesus' presence with others.

Overview

Any exploration of the sacrament of eucharist is not complete if it stops at the eucharistic table on Sunday. The "body of Christ" as represented by the community of the baptized is called to be broken on behalf of others in the world. In fact, the word "Mass" comes from the Latin *Missa*, for "the sending forth of the faithful." Catholics are charged to take the nourishment received at eucharist and feed a world hungering for food for their bodies, minds, and spirits. It is through this practice of service that we grow in our understanding of Christ's "real presence" in eucharist. This session examines several understandings of presence. The Opening Activity allows the participants to share ways people have made their presence felt. In Part I, the participants explore further the meaning of real presence as it relates to eucharist. In Part II, the participants learn how the eucharist is also a sacrifice. Sacrifice—"to make holy"—is explained in the light of Jesus' life and death given on behalf of others. Opportunities to work on a service project help the participants put this call into practice.

Mentor Component

Take note of the service opportunity suggested in Part II. This activity can be extended by having the mentors and teens personally deliver the special gift of a toy and letter to an agency that serves children. Provide addresses of nearby agencies that meet this criterion. Have the participants include any directions of this kind in the Mentor Memo panels.

Session Outline

Opening Activity: Making Your Presence Felt (about 20 minutes)
Part I: What Is Meant by "Real Presence"? (about 45 minutes)
Break (about 5 minutes)
Part II: Sacrifice Means to Make Holy (about 35 minutes)
Prayer Experience: When Did We See You? (about 15 minutes)
Feedback and Conclusion (about 30 minutes)

Supplies

For this session you will need:

- pencils or pens
- extra copies of the Participant Book for guests
- 8 1/2" x 11" pieces of card stock (one for each participant)
- hole punch
- 2-foot pieces of yarn
- dark-colored felt tip markers (one for each participant)
- small box with set of keys hidden inside
- a photo of a family you know well with both parents and at least two children
- a photo of an adopted child you know
- a personal letter or birthday card from a friend
- a knitted sweater or blanket or some other homemade item
- six copies of Resource 9, "The Jesus Show Questions"
- a microphone or similar prop
- letter quality paper
- envelopes
- a variety of empty boxes to wrap gifts in
- gift wrapping paper
- tape
- scissors

- five or six medium-size candles with non-conductive candle holders
- recording of "Our Blessing Cup" by Bob Hurd (OCP Publications) or another similar communion song
- tape or CD player
- copies of Resource 10, "Eucharist Squares" (one for each participant)
- nine copies of Resource 11, "Eucharist Squares Answers"
- feedback slips (3" x 5" slips of paper)

Special Preparations

1. Remind each participant by phone call or letter to bring a toy or other gift for the children who you have arranged to have receive them. The toy should also have special meaning to the participants (see Session Three, Feedback and Conclusion, No. 7).
2. Punch two holes in the top of each piece of card stock. For one piece of card stock, tie the ends of a 2-foot piece of yarn in each hole so that it can be worn around your neck.
3. Prepare two teenagers to enact in front of the group an argument and a reconciling handshake (see Part I, No. 8).
4. Cut "The Jesus Show" Questions (Resource 9) apart and assemble them in stacks so that each participant will receive three or four different questions. Choose an adult or capable teen to play the role of Jesus in the Phil Donahue-style "Jesus Show" (see Part I, No. 12).
5. Arrange for an agency that sponsors young children in need (foster home facility, group home, hospital etc.) or poor families in your neighboring area to accept gifts of new and/or valuable toys for the children in their care. Ask a representative of the agency to attend this session and speak with the teens about the children they serve (optional).

Settings

You will need the following areas for this session:

1. A large area where the participants can gather in a relaxed and comfortable atmosphere for large-group discussions. The room should have an open space from where the participants can easily view a chalkboard or easel and a large supply table to collect toys and other gifts.
2. An area where teens can gather around circular tables in groups of six to eight.
3. An area for the Prayer Experience. This can be handled in the large meeting area. If possible, provide cushions or floor pillows for the participants to sit on during this time.

Opening Activity: Making Your Presence Felt

(about 20 minutes)

Welcome/Check-in

1. Greet the participants as they arrive. Collect the toys and gifts they have brought for children on a large supply table. Ask them to report to tables with their group moderators for attendance and to share their Teen-Mentor Meeting 3 summary and verification signature. Answer any questions on eucharist that you were unable to respond to in Session Three.
2. Pass out pieces of card stock and yarn to each table. Show the card stock with yarn tied through the two holes that you have prepared. Wear the yarn around your neck with the card stock draped down your back. Instruct the participants to make the same type of "billboard" for themselves and put them on.

What Are You Known By?

3. When everyone is finished, call the participants to the large meeting area. Divide the group in half by having them form two circles, one circle inside the other. Ask members of both circles to face inward. (The members of the outside circle should be directly facing the billboards on the back of the members of the inside circle.) If there is an odd number of participants, join one of the circles to make them even. Give the members of the outer circle a felt tip marker. Say, for example:

   This is our fourth session together and we certainly know more about each other than when we first began. How do we think of each other? When this course is over, how will we remember each other? For example, I'll remember Jamie for her strong opinions on her faith. I'll remember Fred for his gold chains. And, among other things, I'll remember you, Heather, for always being late! Outer circle members, for the person in front of you, print a word or short phrase that describes how the person has made his or her presence felt. Please keep your descriptions in good taste.

4. Allow a minute, then call time and have the inner circle members rotate to the right. Repeat the process of writing and moving until the inner circle is back to its original position. Then, ask the members of outer circle to give their markers to the inner circle members. Have both circles face outward and continue the exercise, this time with the inner circle members writing descriptions of the outer circle members.
5. When the exercise is complete, ask the participants to remove their billboards and read the words and phrases that describe how they've made their presence felt, according to their peers. Then ask:

   If you were writing a word or phrase to describe Jesus' presence among you, what would you write?

Call on volunteers to share possible answers (e.g., love, care, service, bread, healing, etc.) Then summarize this activity and introduce the major theme of the session by reading the opening text on page 35 of the Participant Book.

Part I: What Is Meant by "Real Presence"?

(about 45 minutes)

1. Ask the participants to gather near you in the large meeting area. Have them sit on chairs or the floor, preferably in a semicircle. Tell them you are going to talk about the mystery of Jesus' presence in the eucharist, one of the most profound mysteries of our faith. For this presentation, have the actual exhibits ready for display as you explain presence in the different ways. Call on volunteers to respond to the questions for each example.

2. Hold up a small box in which you have secretly placed some keys. Hold it quietly so that the keys don't rattle. Say:

   My keys are present in the box. Do you believe they are there? Why or why not?

   Put the box down with the mystery unsolved.

3. Pass around the photo of the family you know well, and discuss the presence of the parents in each child. Point out physical resemblances. Mention other ways (e.g., personality, behaviors) that the kids are like the mom or dad. Say:

   Someday these parents will no longer be living. Will they still be present in the family? On which occasions will the family be especially aware of their presence? (e.g., holidays, mealtimes, birthdays, etc.).

4. Pass around a photo of an adopted child. Say, for example:

   This is a photo of Jenny, who is adopted. How are adoptive parents present in their adopted children? (e.g., through their love, shared interests, traditions).

5. Pass around the letter or birthday card from a friend. Say, for example:

   This is a personal letter from my friend Mary. What does it mean to say that Mary is present in the letter? What do I have to do to experience her presence? (e.g., read the letter carefully, reflectively).

6. Ask for a show of hands of the teens who have ever baby-sat for a younger child. Call to the front one of the teens with his or her hand up. Say to the person:

   When you are baby-sitting, the parents of the little children are present in you. What does that mean to you? (Pause for response.) What does that mean to the children?

7. Show a homemade sweater or other gift item. Say:

   Suppose a wife knits this sweater (makes this gift) for her husband for Christmas. What does it mean to say that she is present in the gift? How is she more present that if she had bought the sweater?

8. Call the two participants you have prepared for the dramatization of an argument between them. Have them act out the argument. Then say:

   Cut to the next day.

   Have the actors continue with one person admitting to the other person that he or she is at least half at fault and extending a hand as a sign of reconciliation. Ask:

   What does it meant to say that ____name____ is making himself (herself) present in the handshake? (e.g., the handshake is a symbolic sign of the reconciliation).

Exercise

9. Ask the participants to turn to page 36, "Jesus' Presence in the Eucharist." Read the directions and allow a few minutes for marking and writing. Then ask the participants to form triads, give their choices (including reasons for their "best" example), and explain them to one another.

10. Write the seven choices on the board. After the discussion, tally the answers for "best" example. Explain that in one sense all of the answers are right, because each tells something of how Jesus is present in eucharist, but that all the answers are also wrong, because no human example can fully explain the mystery of God's presence in eucharist. Say:

    The church teaches that Jesus is really present in the eucharist in many ways. Look at the list on page 37 of how the *Catechism of the Catholic Church* explains Jesus' presence. Which example from our demonstration does each item most closely correspond to?

    Go over the items on the list on page 37 of the Participant Book one at a time. Call on volunteers to make connections with the examples from the demonstration. Fill in with the information from the following background notes as necessary.

    Background Notes

    1. *Jesus is present in the heart of the individual Christian.* This is something like the adoptive parent's example. Jesus is present in the heart of an individual in somewhat the same way these parents are present to their son or daughter.
    2. *Jesus is present in the community gathered in his name.* This is most like the example of parents in a family. Jesus is with his family, the church, for all time, especially in special occasions like the Mass.
    3. *Jesus is present in the words from scriptures that are read at Mass.* This is like the example of the friend in a letter. To find the person in the writing, the words of scripture must be read or listened to carefully and lovingly.
    4. *Jesus is present in his priest, his official representative.* This is like the baby-sitting example. Even though a person might not be a good

baby-sitter, the authority of the parents still resides in him or her. The parents make that presence possible; the baby-sitter doesn't. Apply this to priesthood.

5. *Jesus is present in the consecrated bread and wine—in the eucharistic species.* This is something like both the example of the homemade gift and the example of the handshake. In each case, the giver is putting himself or herself into something visible and offering it to the receiver as a sign of love, forgiveness, commitment, etc.

The Jesus Show

11. The participants remain in the large meeting area for the following activity. Tell the person you have asked to be Jesus to leave the area and await your introduction. Say:

> A parishioner with Hollywood connections has gotten our group some tickets to the taping of *(Oprah, Geraldo, etc.)* , the highest-rated daytime talk show. Since we will be in the studio audience, the director of the show wants us to be prepared. He has sent over a set of questions the guest host will ask. (Give everyone a pack of questions from Resource 9.) I say guest host because I've received word that subbing for *(Oprah, Geraldo, etc.)* is a man I'm sure you are familiar with. Some say he is the biggest star to ever walk the face of the earth. You know him as Jesus Christ. Spend the next ten minutes or so thinking about your questions and jotting down things you might say to answer them. You may work in groups of two or three if you wish.

12. After the preparation time, bring in "Jesus" with a microphone. Have Jesus walk among the group talk-show style, holding a copy of Resource 9 and asking questions from the sheet. Try to have Jesus ask at least one question of each participant.

Break

(about 5 minutes)

Allow a brief time for a stretch and drink of water. Tell the participants to gather after the break in the large meeting area near the board. During the break, pass out to each table gift wrapping materials (paper, scissors, tape, etc.), pens, letter quality paper, and envelopes.

Part II: Sacrifice Means to Make Holy

(about 35 minutes)

1. After everyone is settled, call on volunteers to share examples of what comes to mind when they hear the word sacrifice (write on board). Add some of the following examples if not mentioned.

Examples

- **Parents sacrifice buying new car to pay for child's school tuition.**
- **Parents of a newborn sacrifice sleep in order to care for baby properly.**
- **An athlete sacrifices free time in order to practice and be on the team.**
- **A teenager sacrifices spending time with friends in order to babysit younger sibling.**

Then, continue from the following script.

Script

2. Usually sacrifice has negative connotations because what is sacrificed is pleasurable and difficult to give up. However, sacrifice actually means "to make holy." Sacrifice motivated by love is an outward expression of God's presence in our lives. Jesus' death is often described as a sacrifice of love. It was the most profound act of self-giving on behalf of others. Because of Jesus' sacrifice, the despicable experience of death was transformed into a holy moment of God's faithful presence.

   The church believes that the sacrifice of Christ's death on the cross and the sacrifice of the eucharist are "one single sacrifice" (*CCC*, No. 1367). The sacrifice is manifested in the words of Jesus: "This is my body which is given up for you" and "This cup which is poured out for you is the New Covenant in my blood."

   At every eucharist we, also, are invited to participate with Jesus in his sacrifice, his self-giving on behalf of others for the reign of God. Every time we receive holy communion we publicly proclaim in both word and action our belief in the body of Christ in all its forms, especially in the very body and blood that were offered as a sacrifice for the forgiveness of our sins.

   When the eucharistic minister holds up the bread and wine for you to receive and says, "the body of Christ" and "the blood of Christ," he or she is really asking if you believe in the profound mystery of the eucharist. When you answer "Amen," you are saying yes in an emphatic way. Then, to seal this commitment, you eat the bread which is the body of Christ. You drink the wine which is the blood of Christ.

   Belief in the eucharist is far more than mere intellectual assent to a mystery. True belief includes a willingness to live in such a way that our lives reflect the presence of Jesus.

   Turn to page 38 in the Participant Book. As I read each question, write the response "Amen." If your faith in that aspect of eucharist is strong, write the word in large letters. If it is weak, write your "Amen" small, and make the writing a prayer that Jesus will increase your faith.

   Do you believe this is the body and blood of Christ offered for you on the cross?

   Do you accept the rest of the people here as the body of Christ?

   Do you want to belong to the body of Christ?

   Are you willing to live like the body of Christ?

   Will you do the work of the body of Christ?

Would you be willing to offer your body and blood for others as Christ did?

The reception of the sacred bread and wine is a sacramental action that is packed with meaning and importance and should therefore be taken seriously. It is no wonder St. Paul wrote, "Examine yourselves, and only then eat of the bread and drink of the cup. For all who eat and drink without discerning the body, eat and drink judgment against themselves" (1 Cor 11:28-29, RSV).

Gifts for Others

3. Point to the table with the gifts for children. Hold up one of the toys and dialogue with the person who brought it about why it holds, or once held, special significance for him or her. For example, ask the person to tell what special memories from his or her own life the toy evokes. Repeat the questioning with one or two other gift-bearers. Say:

   As we learned before, when we give gifts we are in some way sharing part of ourselves with others. We are present to others. Offering part of ourselves to others parallels the gift of sacrifice that Jesus offers to us on the cross and in eucharist. We might have used our money to buy something for ourselves. Instead, we are giving these toys to children we have never met. This is a "sacrifice" in the traditional understanding of "giving something up." When our gift is motivated by love, however, it also "makes us holy"—not a pious kind of holy, but a holiness that goes hand in hand with deep soul happiness.

4. Ask the participants to take their gifts from the supply table and return to the tables with their group moderators. Tell them that they have about twenty minutes to (1) gift-wrap their toy, (2) write a short note to the child (addressed as "Dear Friend") telling something about themselves, why the toy was significant to them, and a wish they have for the child, and (3) tape the sealed envelope on the outside of the package.

5. Arrange for delivery of the gifts to the agency you have selected. See teen-mentor Activity Suggestion 1 on page 41 of the Participant Book for one possibility for delivery.

   Optional: Allow a representative of the agency that will receive the toys to tell the teens about the children they serve.

Prayer Experience: When Did We See You?

(about 15 minutes)

1. Call the participants to the area you have reserved for prayer. Tell them to bring pencils and books, sit in a circle, and open to page 39, "Lord, When Did We See You?" Light the candles and display them on a table as the participants enter the space.

2. Quiet the group. Play a recording of "Our Blessing Cup" by Bob Hurd or the other communion song you have chosen. Ask the participants to concentrate on the

lyrics, imagining that they are being addressed directly to each one of them.

3. Choose an adult or a teen who is a good reader to read aloud the variation of Matthew 25:31-45 on page 39.

4. Ask the participants to print anywhere on the page the first name or initials of persons who have one of the needs described by Jesus. Ask them to think of ways they might be able to help the persons whose names they wrote.

5. Dim the lights in the room. Say:

> You will be moving to separate areas of the room with your group moderator and others in your group. Group moderators, please take one of the lighted candles with you. When you get to your area, form a tight circle sitting on the floor. Then pass the candle around the circle twice. The first time the candle is passed, each person will offer a prayer for one of the persons he or she listed in their books. You do not have to name the person. For example, "For a neighbor who never has any visitors." Everyone responds, "Lord, hear our prayer." The second time the candle goes around, pray in silence, asking God for the strength to help the person in need.
>
> When everyone has been prayed for, put the candle in the center of your group. Each person is to reach out and touch the base with one hand while you pray the Our Father.

Feedback and Conclusion

(about 30 minutes)

Eucharist Squares

1. Conclude the session in the large meeting area. Tell the participants they are going to play a version of the television game show *Hollywood Squares* with questions related to eucharist. Choose nine volunteers as celebrity players and have them face the group, forming three rows for a tic-tac-toe board. (Have three participants sit on the floor, three others sit in chairs behind them, and the final three stand to form the third row.)

2. Divide the rest of the group in half into X and O teams. Give to each of the players in the square one copy of Resource 10, "Eucharist Squares." Give everyone else a copy of Resource 11, "Eucharist Squares Answers." Explain the rules of the game: The object of the game is to win as in tic-tac-toe. And, as in the television game of Hollywood Squares, the players can bluff answers to a question. Point out that for each question, a correct answer and a bluff answer are given on the answer sheet. In order to gain a square, a team must determine whether or not the answer given is a correct one or a bluff by agreeing or disagreeing. A team does not gain a square upon an incorrect response of its opponent.

Optional: Allow the volunteers to choose and print a celebrity name on the back of their copies of Resource 10 and be addressed by this chosen name through the course of the game.

3. Play the game. Alternate between teams. Call on a representative from the X team to choose a square and read the number of the question from the sheet and the question itself. After the celebrity answers the question, allow one minute for the team members to confer. Then call on the representative to share the team's answer (agree or disagree). If right, hand the celebrity a piece of card stock with a printed X to hold for the rest of the game. If wrong, repeat the question and share the correct answer. Repeat the process with an O team representative. Play until a winner is determined. Play a second round if you have time and enough questions.

Follow-up

4. Have the small groups move back to tables. Pass a stack of feedback slips to each table. Ask the participants to complete one or more of the following sentence starters (write on board) and share as time allows with those at their tables:

   One new insight I have gained about eucharist is . . .

   Regarding eucharist, I am still confused about . . .

   I have decided to make a commitment to . . .

Mentor Meeting Reminder

5. Remind the participants of Teen-Mentor Meeting 4. Have them record any information pertaining to one of the Activity Suggestions in the Mentor Memo panel. Remind them to bring their books to their meeting.

6. Remind the participants of the date of the next session. Dismiss the group on time.

Reconciliation: Repairing Our Lives

Session Five

Objectives

The purpose of this session is to help the participants:

- explore the need for reconciliation in various relationships;
- understand the process of healing rooted in the sacrament of reconciliation;
- view the sacrament of reconciliation as a way of encountering the healing and forgiving Lord becoming a similarly reconciling person.

Overview

The reign of God is characterized by people who live in right relationship with themselves, others, their environment, and God. Sin, on the other hand, is brokenness in relationships and a contradiction to God's reign. Jesus is the one who bridges the chasm of sin and offers reconciliation to those who need healing. The process of reconciliation is one that originates in our recognition of our failings and ends with the re-establishment of our communion with others, all done in union with God's grace. This process is enacted in many occasions and in many of our relationships. When enacted sacramentally, we are able in a symbolic way to externalize our desire to improve our lives and reconcile our relationships. The sacrament also provides the power, courage, and resolve we need to really change our lives. The Opening Activity of this session examines many negative ways people choose to handle conflicts in relationship. Part I explores a four-step process of reconciliation that is commonly used to heal brokenness in relationships and which parallels the steps in the sacrament of reconciliation. A personal scripture activity allows the participants to witness examples of forgiveness shared in the gospels. In Part II, the participants are provided with an historical overview of the development of the sacrament of reconciliation and they review some basic actions used in celebrating the sacrament. The participants also have a chance to ask pertinent questions they have about the sacrament of reconciliation.

Mentor Component

Preview Teen-Mentor Meeting 5. Provide a list of the times the sacrament of reconciliation is offered in your parish (see Activity Suggestion 3). You may wish to make this an assigned activity. Have the participants record this and other needed information in the Mentor Memo panel.

Session Outline

Opening Activity: Different Ways to Settle Differences (about 20 minutes)

Part I: A Process of Reconciliation (about 50 minutes)

Break (about 5 minutes)

Prayer Experience: Transforming Our Hurts (about 20 minutes)

Part II: More About Reconciliation (about 45 minutes)

Feedback and Conclusion (about 10 minutes)

Supplies

For this session you will need:

- pencils or pens
- extra copies of the Participant Book
- a large collection of crayons
- bibles
- a large candle
- recording of music that evokes a sense of restlessness and disharmony and a second recording of music that evokes peacefulness
- tape or CD player
- copy of Resource 12, "Reconciliation Speaker Preparation Sheet"
- copies of schedules of reconciliation times at your parish

Special Preparations

1. Cue the recording you have chosen for the Prayer Experience.
2. Arrange for a priest to answer the teen's questions about the sacrament of reconciliation. Provide Resource 12, "Reconciliation Speaker Preparation Sheet," and a copy of the Participant Book to the priest to help him prepare.
3. (optional) If you will offer a celebration of the sacrament of reconciliation for the Prayer Experience (see Prayer Experience, No. 7), you will need to arrange for a sufficient number of priests for individual confessions.

Settings

You will need the following areas for this session:

1. A large area where the participants can gather in a relaxed and comfortable atmosphere for large-group discussions. The room should have an open space from which the participants can easily view a chalkboard or easel.
2. An area where teens can gather around circular tables in groups of six to eight.
3. "Alone" spots—places where the participants can be at least six feet away from everyone else.
4. An area for the Prayer Experience. This can be handled in the large meeting area. If possible, provide cushions or floor pillows for the participants to sit on during this time. A supply table should be positioned in one area of the room.

Opening Activity: Different Ways to Settle Differences

(about 20 minutes)

Welcome/Check-in

1. Greet the participants as they arrive. Ask the teens to report to their group moderators at small group tables for attendance and to share the summaries and verification signatures for Teen-Mentor Meeting 4. Allow time for the teens to report on the activity they completed with their mentors.

Blueprint for Life

2. Pass out a collection of crayons to each table. Tell each person to choose two different colors. Read the first paragraph on page 42. Give the participants directions for coloring the pyramid by naming each word on the pyramid and reading the accompany sentence. Remind them that one color represents primarily good choices in a particular area, the other color primarily bad choices. Go through the following list one at a time. Say:

- Honesty. Do you admit your mistakes or do you blame others?
- Education. Do you value your education or do you goof around and waste lots of time at school?
- Health. Do you take care of your body with proper rest, exercise, and diet or do you abuse it with drugs or alcohol?
- Freedom. Are you free enough to stand up for what you believe or are you blindly led by the crowd?
- Integrity. Are you basically the same person around everyone you meet or are you a fake, changing your behavior depending on who you are with?

- Property. Do you treat things that belong to others with care or do you mistreat or damage the property of others, including public property?
- Sex. Do you show respect for sexuality in your choice of music and entertainment, your jokes and your languages, and your treatment of persons of the opposite gender?
- Environment. Do you protect nature and wildlife or do you litter and pollute with little regard for the place where you live?
- Truth. Do you avoid cheating and other forms of dishonesty or do you use excuses like "everyone does it" to justify dishonest behaviors?
- Respect. Do you respect a person's right to be different or do you tease and belittle others who do not look or behave like you do?
- Words. Do you speak properly and avoid vulgar language or do you speak rudely, including using God's name in vain?
- Trust. Do you put your trust in God's plan for your life or in money, wealth, and other securities?
- Worship. Do you attend and participate in Mass each Sunday and holy day or do you go "only when you feel like it?"
- Creation. Do you respect all of life as a gift of the Creator God or do you treat some—like the unborn, sick, or elderly—as less important?
- Prayer. Do you take time to talk to God at various times of the day or do you "go it alone" without ever thinking about God?

3. Summarize the activity and introduce the theme of the session by reading the second paragraph on page 42.

Part I: A Process of Reconciliation

(about 50 minutes)

1. Read the directions for the Journal Activity on page 43, "Handling Conflicts." Ask the participants to work in alone spots to finish each of the sentences. Allow about ten minutes for writing. Then call everyone to the large meeting area near the board and ask volunteers to share some of the strategies they listed for settling conflicts in each of the areas. Summarize on the board and list some of the negative ways for handling conflicts. Add the following to the list if not named by the group:

    - **Retaliation**. Some people handle conflicts by "getting even." Someone calls them a bad name; they retaliate by doing the same. They aren't invited to a classmate's party; they retaliate by not inviting that person the next time they hold a party.
    - **Blaming**. "It's your fault, not mine." Blaming the other person is another way people choose to handle conflicts in relationships.
    - **Avoiding.** When a conflict arises, some avoid or ignore its causes altogether. The relationship may continue, but the problem is never mentioned again, though it remains simmering below the surface.

When a volunteer mentions a positive way of handling conflicts, especially strategies like **talking things out, forgiveness, listening,** and **reconciliation,** write them in a separate corner of the board but avoid talking about them until all of the negative ways for handling conflicts are exhausted. Then, begin a presentation on a process of reconciliation based on the following script.

Script

2. How effective is retaliation for handling conflicts? A war of insults, barbs, or disparaging words may end the conflict. Unfortunately, the relationship itself would likely end too.

   In the blaming approach, all energy becomes focused on defending one's own position rather than working to solve the problem. Though there might be some satisfaction in clearing the air and expressing one's anger, it's unlikely the relationship will be able to survive.

   Avoiding a conflict is sometimes a good strategy, especially if one person fears physical or emotional dangers from confronting another. However, even in that situation, a person should make efforts to settle the conflict internally (e.g., through talking the situation out with a trusted third party) so that the problem does not fester and cause anger to build up inside.

   Let's take a look at a process that works toward both settling conflicts and restoring relationships when sinful choices are involved. It is the process rooted in the sacrament of reconciliation. (Remember, a sin is a deliberate choice to turn away from God or to break God's law.)

   The first step is **become aware that you have offended** (write on the board, beginning a new column). It involves questioning yourself for all areas of your life, not just the situation in question. You ask yourself: How am I treating others? How am I contributing to my family's well-being? How am I following God's commandments? Call on the Holy Spirit to help you ask and answer these questions. Also, consider if any of your choices have been sinful.

   The next step is probably the most difficult. You **admit your fault** (write) to the offended person. You tell the person what you did. If you lie to one friend about being busy so that you could go out with a second friend, you confess to the first friend by telling what you did and admitting your fault.

   You also **express your sorrow** (write). You tell the person you are sorry for doing what you did. The words "I am sorry" disarm people and help to remove of their defenses. It's very likely that the other person will also apologize for his or her part in the conflict, if warranted, besides accepting your apology. If he or she does so, you have been offered **forgiveness** (write).

   After you have been forgiven you try to **change your conduct** (write). A person you hurt may have an idea for how you can do better. The friend who was stood up might insist that you promise to make it up by going out together on the next weekend. If you talked back to your parents you can make up for it by being extra kind and helpful. If you cheated by copying another person's assignment, you could make it up redoing your own version of the assignment.

   This entire process is known as **reconciliation** (write at the top of the column). To reconcile means to "re-establish your once-close relationship." The elements of this process are present in the sacrament of reconciliation. They go by different names, but the process is the same. "Becoming aware you have offended" is also known as an **examination of conscience** (write next to the first item). **Confession** (write next to second item) is another name for "admitting your fault." **Contrition** (write) is a word that means "to express sorrow." In the sacrament of reconciliation, the priest prays a prayer of **absolution** (write)—"to take away sin"—when you are forgiven. The name for "changing your conduct" is **penance** (write). The priests usually has some suggestions for things you can do. This process of reconciliation is also found in gospel stories where Jesus offers or speaks about forgiveness. Jesus sought out people and situations that needed the hand of a reconciler, the hand of God. He didn't always wait for a person to come to him. Let's see how the elements of this process are present in the gospels.

Scripture Exercise

3. Give everyone a bible and have them move to alone spots with their bibles, books, and pens. Say:

   Page 44 lists five scripture passages that involve reconciliation. When I finish talking I would like you to look up and read the first passage prayerfully and attentively, the famous parable of the lost son from Luke 15:11-32. After you've read the passage once all the way through, go back and look for examples of elements of the reconciliation process (also listed on page 44). Write which steps are evident in each passage. Explain how they are evident.

   Quiet yourselves now. Ask Jesus to speak to you through the words of the gospels. You can open the bible and begin. When you've completed the first passage, move on to the others.

4. Allow about twenty minutes for reading and writing, depending on the reflectiveness of the group. Then ask them to form in groups of three in the large meeting area. Say:

   Take turns discussing your insights for each passage. Explain for your group the element of the reconciliation process that particularly stood out for you or present a question you had for a passage and ask the others to respond.

5. After a few minutes for discussion, take the participants through the chart on page 45, "A Movement of Healing," summarizing the scripture exercise by pointing out how the reconciliation process shared by Jesus in the gospels parallels the process in the sacrament of reconciliation.

Panel Discussion

6. Call everyone to the large meeting area. Use the panel method of discussion (see Appendix, page 121) to identify situations and relationships that can benefit from the process of reconciliation. Use the following questions as a starting point, but ad-lib as the conversation dictates and add some other questions of your own. You may wish to select a second panel halfway through the discussion. Dialogue in this format for about fifteen minutes.

Questions

- What is the major source of conflict between you and your parents?
- What is the longest you've gone without speaking to one of your parents? What was the reason for this?
- Who finds it more difficult to say "I'm sorry:" you or your parents? Why do you think this is so?
- What's the worst thing a friend ever did to you? Was this problem resolved? How so?
- Is there something a friend could do to you that you could never consider forgiving? Explain.
- Have you ever had someone confess to you that they had hurt you? What did they do that helped you accept the confession or that made it difficult to accept their apology?
- If you honestly examined your conscience regarding your performance at school, what is one conclusion you would come up with?
- Do you have built-in reminders to examine your conscience regularly? Do you take advantage of them? What are some ways you could plan regularly to examine your conscience?
- What is the difference between a sin and a mistake?
- Do you think it is possible to offend God? How so?
- Have you ever had anyone reject your apology? Why do you think this happened?
- How can this reconciliation process help different racial or cultural groups to a better relationship?
- What do you think you would say to a friend who told you about an abortion she had and now felt guilty about? What might a process of reconciliation look like in this case?
- Which of God's commandments do you find most difficult to follow? Why?
- What do you do when you commit a sin?
- What is an example of penance you have witnessed depicted in literature or the movies? In that example, how was the penance a part of the larger process of reconciliation?
- Who is someone you know whose acceptance of you frees you to be able to say "I am sorry" more easily? When have you been accepting of others in this way?

Break

(about 5 minutes)

Allow about five minutes for a stretch, drink of water, etc. Make final preparations for the prayer space. Tell the participants to meet after the break in the area you have prepared. Prepare a participant to read John 14:23-27 for the Prayer Experience.

Prayer Experience: Transforming Our Hurts

(about 20 minutes)

1. Ask the participants to form a circle and sit on the floor. Dim the lights as the participants enter the prayer space. Play the music that you have chosen that evokes a sense of restlessness or disharmony. Light a candle and place it in the center of the circle.

2. Say:

   Take a moment to remember a time you have been hurt or a time you have hurt someone else: a harsh word exchanged with a parent, a physical hurt you experienced or caused, a time you were snubbed or made fun of. Remind yourself of what happened, how it felt to you then, how it felt to others, how it feels now.

3. Call on a reader you have chosen to read John 14:23-27.

4. Say:

   Let us pray for the healing of our hurts and the acceptance of the healing peace offered by Jesus. As we go around the circle, let us lift up our own personal hurts and the hurts of the world. You may mention your own hurt or a hurt in society like war, gang violence, racism, or discrimination. Or you may simply offer your prayer in silence. Our response is "Heal us, Lord." (Start the prayer around the circle so they know how to proceed: "For ___name of hurt___, we pray . . . heal us, Lord.")

5. Instruct the person on your right to continue the prayer. When everyone has shared, tell the participants to stand. Ask each person to face another, placing his or her right hand on the other person's shoulder. Pray an Our Father. Then, add:

   Lord Jesus Christ, you said to your apostles: I leave you peace, my peace I give you. Look not on our sins, but on the faith of your church, and grant us the peace and unity of your kingdom where you live for ever and ever. (Response: Amen.)

   The peace of the Lord be with you always. (Response: And also with you.)

   Let us offer each other the sign of peace.

6. After the participants exchange greetings, ask them to sit again in the circle. Play a recording of uplifting, peaceful music. Say:

   As the music plays, imagine being healed from the hurt you remembered before. What does it feel like to you to have that pain healed? What steps must you take to be reconciled to someone else?

   Allow two or three minutes or for the song to end. Then ask the participants to stand, face the center of the circle. Pray (from the Rite of Penance):

   May the God of peace
   fill your hearts with every blessing.

May he sustain you
with his gifts of hope and consolation,
help you to offer your lives in his service,
and bring you safely to eternal glory.
May almighty God,
(lead sign of the cross) the Father, and the Son, and the Holy Spirit,
grant you all that is good.
Amen.

7. Ask the participants to return to their table groups with their group moderators. ***Optional:*** Offer the opportunity for celebration of the sacrament of reconciliation. You may use the Prayer Experience as an opening communal prayer before allowing the participants the opportunity for individual confessions. Station the priest(s) at alone spots throughout the large meeting area.

Part II: More About Reconciliation

(about 45 minutes)

1. When everyone is seated, refer to the Prayer Experience. Say:

In prayer, we did a lot of "hands-on" things. We named a hurt, prayed for its removal, and transformed it into an area of healing by offering each other peace through the laying on of hands. Using hands and touch in a ritual of reconciliation has always been very natural to human beings. Think of the times you reconcile with others: hugs, handshakes, a pat on the back, or a gentle touch are ways of saying that the hurt is forgiven and you are ready to restore peace in your relationship. For the church, the sacrament of reconciliation is and always has been a hands-on experience of God's forgiving love which restores us to communion with God and one another, and empowers us to offer the same love to others.

Take some time to examine the four brief sketches of the sacrament of reconciliation on pages 46-47. Then think about and finish the sentences on page 47. You will be asked to share what you write with others at your table.

2. Allow fifteen minutes for reading and writing. Then read the first sentence starter. Designate the person wearing the most green in each group to finish the sentence for others at the table. Allow time for everyone to go around the tables and share. Repeat the process for the other sentence-starters.

3. Limit the total discussion time to about ten to fifteen minutes. Then explain to the participants that you have invited a priest to give a brief talk about the sacrament of reconciliation and that he has reserved time at the end of his presentation to answer their questions. Tell them to think of two or three questions and write them in the space at the bottom of page 47.

Guest Speaker Presentation

4. Have the participants gather in the large meeting area. Welcome the priest. Remind him that you have reserved ten to fifteen minutes at the end of his presentation for the participants to ask the questions they have prepared.

   Optional: If you have not been able to arrange a guest speaker, you can address as many as you can of the questions the participants have formed. Write down questions you can't answer and promise you will find out an answer before the next session. Also, spend some time reviewing the different names (taken from the *Catechism of the Catholic Church*) of the sacrament on page 48 of the Participant Book.

Feedback and Conclusion

(about 10 minutes)

Role Play

1. Set up two chairs facing one another in front of the group. Ask for two volunteers to take the parts of priest and penitent and briefly role play these main elements of the sacrament of reconciliation: (1) welcome, (2) sharing of scripture, (3) confession of sins, (4) act of contrition, (5) absolution, (6) giving of penance, and (7) sending. Choose more volunteers to repeat the role play as time allows.

Mentor Meeting Reminder

2. Remind the participants of Teen-Mentor Meeting 5. Have them record any information pertaining to one of the activity suggestions in the Mentor Memo panel. Pass out schedules of reconciliation times at your parish. Remind them to bring their books to their meeting.
3. Dismiss the group on time.

Anointing the Sick: Healing the Pain

session Six

Objectives

The purpose of this session is to help the participants:

- empathize with the experience of suffering and illness;
- discover Jesus' response to suffering and the ministry of healing of the early church;
- understand the place of the sacrament of the anointing of the sick within the context of total ministry to the sick.

Overview

Suffering due to physical, mental, emotional, and spiritual illness is part of the human condition. Whether we are temporarily out of commission with the flu or seriously ill with a life-threatening disease, sickness can claim our total being. It is an experience that can separate us from our usual self-identity and from one another. Empathy is a first step in offering healing to the suffering lives of others. In this session, the participants reflect on the suffering that has been a part of their own lives and learn to empathize with the suffering of others. They consider the question "Why suffering?" and see what response was offered by Jesus. The participants also reflect on and write their responses to several contemporary situations that involve suffering. In Part II, the participants examine the elements of the sacrament of the anointing of the sick and see how their call of discipleship includes a challenge to continue Jesus' ministry of healing.

Mentor Component

Preview Teen-Mentor Meeting 6. Each of the activity suggestions requires scheduling and planning. Make sure to communicate the necessary details to the participants. Have them record the information in the Mentor Memo panels.

session Six

Session Outline

Opening Activity: Feeling the Pain (about 25 minutes)
Part I: Jesus' Answer to Suffering (about 50 minutes)
Break (about 5 minutes)
Part II: The Sacrament of Anointing the Sick (about 40 minutes)
Prayer Experience: Extending Christ's Healing Hands (about 20 minutes)
Feedback and Conclusion (about 10 minutes)

Supplies

For this session you will need:

- pencils or pens
- extra copies of the Participant Book
- a copy of the video *Superman: The Movie*, starring Christopher Reeve
- VCR and monitor
- bibles
- letter quality paper
- envelopes
- names and addresses of sick or homebound parishioners
- 3" x 5" slips of paper
- display table
- olive oil for anointing of hands
- tissue paper or towels
- bowl with water
- three floating candles
- felt squares in a variety of colors
- felt markers
- scissors
- recording of "The Last Song" by Elton John or "Lay Your Hands" by Carey Landry
- tape or CD player

Special Preparations

1. Cue a five-minute segment from *Superman: The Movie*, including an action-packed scene where Superman saves the day.
2. Print the names and addresses of sick or homebound parishioners on separate 3" x 5" slips of paper. Make sure to have one card for each participant. Repeat names and addresses as necessary. Note the suggestions for delivery of the letters to the sick in Part II, No. 6.
3. Prepare a teen to read Mark 3:1-6 for the Prayer Experience.

Settings

You will need the following areas for this session:

1. A large area where the participants can gather in a relaxed and comfortable atmosphere for large-group discussions. The room should have an open space from which the participants can easily view a chalkboard or easel.
2. An area where teens can gather around circular tables in groups of six to eight.
3. "Alone" spots—places where the participants can be at least six feet away from everyone else.
4. An area for the Prayer Experience. It's best to be able to convert the large meeting area into a space for prayer for this session. Set up a display table with the prayer items (oil, bowl of water, floating candles, and bible) in one corner of the room until it is needed.

Opening Activity: Feeling the Pain

(about 25 minutes)

Welcome/Check-in

1. As the participants arrive, ask them to take a pair of scissors, a marker, and a felt square and report to a table with their group moderators for attendance and to show the summary and verification signature from Teen-Mentor Meeting 5. Next, ask them to trace and cut out their hand from the felt square. When all have done this, say:

> On your felt hand, print the first name or initials of someone you know who is sick, elderly, or suffering. Keep the felt hand pressed in the back pages of your book. We'll be using it as part of our prayer experience later in the session.

Introduction

2. Gather everyone in the large meeting space with their books and pens. Write and explain the following term and definition on the board:

Empathy: identification with and understanding of another's situation, feelings, and motives.

Read or have the participants individually read the introductory story about Elaine on pages 51-52. Then conduct a discussion with the entire group, using the following questions to identify how the characters in the story had empathy for each other.

Questions

- Who did Elaine show empathy for? How?
- How did Elaine's mom and aunt show empathy for her?
- What do you think were some positive benefits of empathy in these situations?

3. After the discussion, introduce the main focus of the session by reading or summarizing the final paragraph on page 52.

Journal Activity

4. Ask the participants to move to alone spots to complete the Journal Activity on page 53. Allow about ten minutes for writing. Then call everyone back to their table groups. Say:

> Choose one of the responses you feel most comfortable talking about with your group. Go around the table sharing that response. The person with the most buttons on his or her shirt goes first.

5. When everyone has had a chance to share, summarize the Opening Activity. Say:

> When you first arrived you cut out a hand from felt and wrote your name on it. Our hands symbolize our efforts to reach out and offer healing to one another. Let's take a look at a way we can do that—empathize and act—when we need to bring healing to others.

Part I: Jesus' Answer to Suffering

(about 50 minutes)

Video Clip

1. Gather the participants around the television monitor and show the video clip that you have prepared from *Superman: The Movie*. After the clip, say:

> It's natural human tendency to wish you were a person of steel and that no harm could come your way. Each time we are ill or injured we are reminded of the fragile nature of human life. The *Catechism of the Catholic Church* points out that in illness we experience our powerlessness, limitations, and finitude. "Every illness can make us glimpse death" (*CCC*, 1501).
>
> In fact, you probably are aware of the story of Christopher Reeve, the actor who portrayed Superman in the movie. In 1995, Reeve was preparing for a horse riding competition when his horse suddenly stopped short, thrusting him over the front of the horse headfirst into the ground. The impact crushed his vertebrae and injured his spinal cord. Reeve was left a quadriplegic—without the use of his entire body below his shoulders—and unable to breathe without the use of a respirator.
>
> A split-second event changed Reeve's life forever. The injury was devastating not only to Reeve's body, but his spirit as well. He credited the love and support of his children and wife for improving his outlook and allowing him to look positively to the future.

Nevertheless, unexpected injuries like Reeve's, terminal illnesses, birth defects, and other sufferings of this type, remind us of perennial human questions: Why is there suffering? and **What is the meaning of suffering?** (write). For Christians, a third question is "What did Jesus say and do about suffering?"

Scripture Exercise

2. Pass out bibles to each person and have them work with a partner to complete the scripture exercise on page 54. Allow ten to fifteen minutes. Call the group together and go over the answers to each part.

   Answers

   1A. Peter's mother-in-law lay sick with a fever.

   1B. Jesus grasped her hand and helped her up.

   1C. The fever left her and she waited on them.

   2A. A man was paralyzed.

   2B. Jesus forgave the man sins and commanded the illness to leave him.

   2C. The man got up and walked home. The witnesses praised God.

   3A. A man had leprosy.

   3B. Jesus touched him and said some words over him.

   3C. The man was immediately healed. Against Jesus' wishes, he publicized the healing to all.

   4A. A mother's only son had died.

   4B. Jesus touched the coffin and commanded the dead man to rise.

   4C. The dead man began to speak. The witnesses were fearful, but began to glorify God.

3. Refer back to the questions on the board. Ask which of the gospel stories in the scripture exercise answered either of the questions. Allow the participants to conclude that in none of these stories does Jesus provide a clear answer about the origins or meaning of suffering. Then continue with a presentation based on the following script.

Script

4. Rather than offer answers to questions about suffering, Jesus approached the issue in a different way. A common pattern, as seen in the scripture stories, was as follows:

   First, Jesus **encountered** (write) the suffering. This in itself was a risky task. Fevers and leprosy are contagious; the latter, especially, life-threatening. Also, Jesus encountered not only the illness, but all of the pain surrounding it. For example, Jesus addressed the paralytic's sinfulness. The raising of the dead man was as much of a response to the sorrow of the man's mother as it was to the need of the man to be resuscitated.

   Second, Jesus **healed** (write) the suffering. He did not offer long discourses about why the person was experiencing the suffering or the meaning of the suffering for the person's life. Rather, he simply healed the person. The signs of Jesus' healing were his words and touch.

Third, there was a **response** (write) by the person who was healed and a response by the witnesses to Jesus' healing actions. This responses took the form of praise for God, a change in life, and a desire to become a follower of Jesus.

Brainstorming

5. Ask the participants to brainstorm examples of illness or suffering they have witnessed in their school and local neighborhood. Write a list of the examples on the board.

Examples

- **a fellow student with a physical handicap**
- **a lonely teen who doesn't seem to have many friends**
- **a classmate who is ridiculed**
- **a neighborhood family without enough food or proper clothing**
- **an older person with severe arthritis**
- **a mother or father who is unemployed**
- **a homeless person begging for food**
- **an innocent child injured due to gang violence**
- **a teen or young adult who is HIV positive**
- **a neighbor with cancer**

Activity

6. Have the participants meet again with their partner. Tell them to turn to page 55, "My Response to Suffering." Give the following directions for completing the chart. Say:

First, work individually and write in the first column three examples of illness or suffering you have personally encountered. You can choose one or more items from the list on the board. (Allow time for writing.)

Next, in the second column, write how you offered healing for the illness or suffering or would offer healing if you encountered this type of illness or suffering again. (Allow time for writing.)

Now, exchange books with your partner. Take the role of the person listed for your partner's first example and imagine the healing offered in column two. What would be your response to this type of healing? Write your response in the third column in your partner's book. Repeat the same process for the other two examples.

7. After everyone has finished writing, have them retrieve their books and read over the responses. Tell them to seek clarification, as needed, for any of the responses.

Summary

8. Ask the participants to meet again near the board. Summarize Part I of the session. Say:

For the most part, Jesus did not spend a lot of time answering questions about suffering. The only answer Jesus gave about the origins of suffering and the meaning of suffering is found in the gospel of John. Encountering a man blind since birth, his disciples asked Jesus, "Rabbi, who sinned, this man or his parents that he was born blind?" Jesus answered: "Neither he nor his parents sinned; it is so that the works of God might be made visible through him" (9:2-3). Jesus then healed the man. The man later witnessed to his cure on Jesus' behalf.

As disciples of Jesus, we are called to follow the example of both Jesus and the man born blind. We are to bring the healing words and touch of Jesus to those who suffer. And when we ourselves benefit from healing words and touch or when we witness a healing in another, we are to offer God our praise and thanksgiving.

Break

(about 5 minutes)

Allow a brief time for a stretch and drink of water. Tell the participants to bring their books and pencils and meet near the board after the break.

Part II: The Sacrament of Anointing the Sick

(about 40 minutes)

1. Draw on the board a version of the "Sacraments Timeline" from page 56 of the Participant Book on the board. Present the history of the sacrament of the anointing of the sick based on the following script. Print the highlighted words on the board near the corresponding years on the timeline. Instruct the participants to print the words in their books as you go along.

Script

2. **Jesus Shares His Healing Ministry** (write on board at approximately A.D. 30) By the time the twelve apostles were commissioned by Jesus, they were charged with his ministry of healing and care for the sick. The gospel of Mark reports that the apostles "anoint-

ed with oil many who were sick and cured them" (6:11). After Jesus rises from the dead, he tells the remaining eleven that they "will lay hands on the sick, and they will recover" (Mk 16:18).

Blessed Oil (write on board at approximately 200) The church continued its official ministry of healing. The Letter of James tells how elders of the church were called to pray over the sick and anoint them with oil. (Read James 5:14-16.) Olive oil was the common oil of Palestine in these days. The oil, blessed by the bishop, was applied to the injured area of the sick person. If it were a general illness, the head, chest, or shoulders were anointed. For emotional or spiritual illnesses, the five senses were anointed. Sometimes the oil was even drunk. During this early period, it is believed that any Christian could anoint another with these blessed oils.

Viaticum (write on board at approximately 700) Up to the eighth century, the emphasis of the sacrament remained on physical and spiritual healing for the sick person. Christians were anointed with oil more than once. The final sacrament for the dying during this time was most frequently *viaticum*, a Latin word that means "food for the journey." This was a dying person's final reception of holy communion.

Extreme Unction (write on board at approximately 1200) After the ninth century, the sacrament became more formally organized. Because some people were assigning false magical value to the oil, only a priest could preside at the sacrament. The sacrament also became associated with the sacrament of penance. And, since penance was generally reserved only for those who had been excommunicated or were near death, the emphasis of the sacrament of anointing changed from healing to a preparation for death. The sacrament became known as *extreme unction*, or "the last anointing."

Council of Trent (write on board at approximately 1500 as a heading for the notes below) The Council of Trent in the sixteenth century taught that anointing the sick was a true sacrament. The Council also affirmed the effects of the sacrament: **(1) forgiveness of sins, (2) healing of the soul and also the body if that is God's will, and (3) union with Christ's suffering.**

Second Vatican Council (write on board at approximately 2000) The Second Vatican Council in the 1960s re-emphasized the ancient practice of anointing with oil and laying hands on any who suffer serious illness—including, the elderly, those facing major surgery, children with a serious illness—as well as the dying. The sacrament is no longer thought of as the "last rites" and can be repeated as many times as necessary. The Council also recommended that the sacrament be celebrated communally when possible, especially within a Sunday liturgy. When the sacrament is celebrated in a home or at the hospital, the sick person's family and friends are encouraged to be present.

The Sacrament Today

3. Explain that whether celebrated within Mass, in a church, outside of Mass, or in a home or hospital, the sacrament has a common outline as listed on page 57, "Rites of the Sacrament." Go through the outline, pointing out how the words and actions of the sacrament are comparable to how Jesus treated sick and suffering people, and comparing the words and actions of the sacrament with what is usually experienced by a sick person.

Letters of Care

4. Explain that the new rite for anointing of the sick also stresses the care of the sick outside of the sacrament itself. Ask:

   What are some ways that you can participate in healing the pain or illness of another?

   Brainstorm with the group several possibilities. Print the suggestions on the board. For example:

   - **Visiting grandparents and older relatives**
   - **Taking school assignments to classmates who are**
   - **Helping physically disabled persons**
   - **Praying regularly for the needs of the sick**
   - **Visiting the sick in hospitals or nursing homes**

5. If the option has not been mentioned, add to the list **writing letters to the sick or homebound.** Then give directions for the letter-writing assignment. Pass out to each participant one 3" x 5" card with the name of a sick or homebound parishioner, letter quality paper, and an envelope. Ask them to use some or all of the letter-writing tips on page 57 to help them write a "letter of care" to the person whose name they were given. Tell them to seal and address the envelope after they have finished writing.

6. Choose one of the following options for delivering the letters:
   1. Assign the participants to deliver the letter in person accompanied by their mentors as suggested in Activity Suggestion 2 on page 59 of the Participant Book. If you choose this option you will need to provide phone numbers so that the sick person can be prepared for the visit.
   2. Invite a member of the parish pastoral care team to come to this session and address the teens on how ministry to the sick is carried out in the parish. Ask this person to have the letters delivered as part of the ministry team's regular rounds.
   3. Mail the letters yourself. Ask the participants to donate the amount of money needed for the stamps.

Prayer Experience:
Extending Christ's Healing Hands

(about 20 minutes)

1. Move to the area you have prepared for prayer. Have the participants bring their felt cut-out hands and sit around the display table. Light the floating candles and dim the lights in the room. Say:

Let this light and water help us recall that Jesus is light of the world and that through our baptism we belong to him.

As we gather, we remember the words written by the apostle James: "Is anyone among you suffering? He should pray. Is anyone in good spirits? He should sing praise. Is anyone among you sick? He should summon the presbyters of the church, and they should pray over him and anoint him with oil in the name of the Lord, and the prayer of faith will save the sick person, and the Lord will raise him up."

Let us listen to the following words from the gospel of Mark.

Gospel Reading

2. Call on the reader you have prepared to read Mark 3:1-6. Then, offer a brief comment on the reading. Say:

How are we like the man with the withered hand? How does our apathy, fear, embarrassment, or helplessness keep us from reaching out to others in need? How are we like the adversaries of Jesus in the story? Do we ourselves believe that the problems of the world are too big for our personal efforts to have any consequence? Like the man with the withered hand, let us reach out to Jesus so that our hands and hearts might be renewed, so that we can bring Jesus' healing touch to those in need.

Anointing

3. Ask the participants to come forward one at a time and anoint one hand of each person. (Ask an adult to help you if the size of the group is too large.) Play the music you have chosen as the anointing takes place.

Intercessions

4. When everyone has returned to their seats, have them hold their felt hands. Go around the circle, asking them to pray aloud for the needs of the person they have printed on the hand using these or similar words:

For ___*name*___ who suffers from ___*type of illness*___ we pray,

Lord Jesus, heal us.

Closing

5. After everyone has prayed, ask the participants to stand around the table and place their felt hands around the bowl of water and candles. Pray together an Our Father. Then close with these words:

Lord, we offer you the prayers and caring of this community for your people in need of healing. Be with us always, and heal us of all that keeps us from being one with you. May we always be your hands to those in need. We ask this in your name.

Amen.

Feedback and Conclusion

(about 10 minutes)

1. Have the participants sit with their table groups. Pass out 3" x 5" slips to each table. Tell the participants to finish one sentence for each slip of paper as time allows. Have the group moderators collect the slips and give them to you after the session. Use them to help evaluate the session. Write the following sentence starters on the board:

   This lesson made sense to me because . . .

   This lesson didn't make sense to me because . . .

   One new thing I learned about the sacrament of anointing the sick is . . .

Mentor Meeting Reminder

2. Preview Teen-Mentor Meeting 6 (pages 58-59 in the Participant Book). Offer specific directions as needed. Remind them to take their books to the meeting and to complete the summary information.
3. Remind the participants of the date of Session Seven. Dismiss them on time.

Holy Orders: A Call to Leadership

Session Seven

Objectives

The purpose of this session is to help the participants:

- understand the roles and functions of bishops, priests, and deacons as lifestyles of service;
- see how symbols of servant leadership are emphasized in the sacrament of holy orders;
- trace the history of ordained leadership and consider questions concerning the ordained ministry for now and the future.

Overview

This session and the next address another movement in Christ which the church celebrates sacramentally. The *Catechism of the Catholic Church* calls the sacraments of holy orders and matrimony "sacraments at the service of communion." These are sacraments that are directed toward the service of others: "They confer a particular mission in the Church and serve to build up the People of God" (*CCC*, #1534). In this session, the sacrament of holy orders is explored, including its main characteristics, its history, and its implications for the community today. Holy orders is an apostolic ministry that includes three degrees: the episcopate, the presbyterate, and the diaconate. In the Opening Activity, the participants attempt to come up with a functional job description for a bishop, priest, and deacon in a particular diocese and parish. In Part I, the qualities of ordained leadership, as represented in the sacrament of holy orders, are explored. Part II covers the history of ordained leadership in the church and the realities associated with accepting a call to an ordained vocation. Opportunity is also provided for the participants to form and share questions they have about the future of ordained ministries and leadership in the church.

Session Seven

Mentor Component

Preview Teen-Mentor Meeting 7 in the Participant Book. Note the activity suggestions. For Activity Suggestion 1, have a local or national Catholic directory on hand as a source for names and addresses of diocesan or religious community vocation directors. If any mentors will be attending this session, plan to welcome them and assign them to a group with their teen partners.

Session Outline

Opening Activity: Qualifications for Church Leaders (about 35 minutes)

Part I: Qualities of Servant Leadership (about 50 minutes)

Break (about 5 minutes)

Prayer Experience: Ministers of Good News (about 15 minutes)

Part II: Church Structure: Events and Issues (about 40 minutes)

Conclusion (about 5 minutes)

Supplies

For this session you will need:

- pencils or pens
- extra copies of the Participant Book
- small dot stickers (four different colors)
- several large skeins of yarn
- bibles (one for each table)
- textbook or periodical resources with information about ordained ministers and the sacrament of holy orders
- copy of Resource 13, "Ordained Ministry Speaker Preparation Sheet"
- recording or lyrics for "Seed, Scattered and Sown" by Dan Felten (Ekklesia Music, IN)
- tape or CD player (optional)
- planter box filled with soil
- candle
- poppy seeds or another type of seed that will grow easily in planter box

Special Preparations

1. For the Opening Activity, using yarn and masking tape, mark off the floor in the large meeting area into six sections covering one side of the room to the other. The floor should look like this:

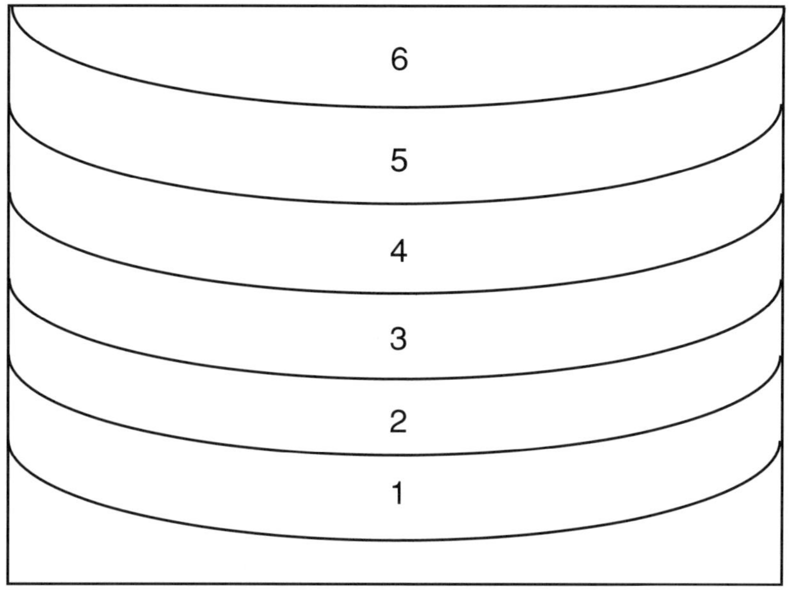

2. Arrange for an ordained minister (priest, deacon, or bishop) to speak for ten minutes about his vocation to ordained ministry. To assist him with preparation, provide him with Resource 13, "Ordained Ministry Speaker Preparation Sheet," prior to the session.

Settings

You will need the following areas for this session:

1. A large area where the participants can gather in a relaxed and comfortable atmosphere for large-group discussions. The room should have an open space from which the participants can easily view a chalkboard or easel.
2. An area where teens can gather around circular tables in four equal-size groups.
3. "Alone" spots—places where the participants can be at least six feet away from everyone else.
4. An area for the Prayer Experience. It's best to be able to convert the large meeting area into a space for prayer for this session. Place a candle and the large container with sand on the floor in the center of the prayer space. Light the candle as the participants enter the space during the prayer time.

Opening Activity: Qualifications for Church Leaders

(about 35 minutes)

Welcome

1. As the participants arrive, randomly distribute the four colors of dot stickers, making sure to end up with groups of equal size. Tell the participants to attach their sticker any place on page 60 and gather in the large meeting area.

Quiz Game

2. Stand on one side of the room. Ask all the participants to stand and form a line across the opposite side of the room in an area you have designated section 1. Tell them they are going to take a brief pre-test on the session topic, holy orders. Say:

I am going to read some questions and statements with two possible answers. Hold up one finger (not your middle finger) if you think number one is the right answer. Hold up two fingers if you think number two is the right answer. When you are correct, you get to move to the next section. If incorrect, stay where you are. The first people to reach my section are the winners!

Use the following multiple choice questions and statements for the game. Add some of your own. Save some difficult ones for the final rounds or to break ties. At the end of the game, lead a round of applause for the winner(s).

Sample Questions and Statements (*indicates correct answers)

- The name of our diocesan (or deanery) bishop is (1) Pope John Paul II or (2)* (share the actual name).
- The National Conference of Catholic Bishops is the association of all bishops of (1)* the United States or (2) of the world.
- The pope is the bishop of (1)* Rome or (2) Krakow.
- The word apostle means (1) bishop or (2)* "one sent."
- In the first century some women served as deacons: (1)* true or (2) false.
- A deacon may be the principal celebrant of a baptism: (1)* true or (2) false.
- Most priests are required to complete four years of graduate study after college: (1)* true or (2) false.
- A man can be a Jesuit and not be ordained: (1)* true or (2) false.
- A religious priest owes his obedience to a (1) bishop or (2)* superior.
- A diocesan priest is also called (1)* a secular priest or (2) a religious priest.
- A nun receives the sacrament of holy orders (1) true or (2)* false.
- A single man who becomes a permanent deacon may later get married: (1) true or (2)* false.

Grouping

3. Designate four tables by "sticker colors" and ask the participants to report to the appropriate places. Read or summarize the opening text on page 60.

Job Qualification Survey

4. Write on the board as headings for separate columns the names of the following job positions as on page 61:

CEO of Diocese

Parish Administrator

Principal of Catholic High School

Hospital Chaplain

Explain the directions for filling out the columns. Say:

> Work with your table group to come up with a list of five qualifications for each job position. For example, one qualification for a CEO of a diocese or an administrator of a parish might be "administrative skills." Qualifications for a school principal and a hospital chaplain might be degrees in education and counseling respectively. Be as specific as possible.

5. Allow ten to fifteen minutes for the groups to complete the chart. Then, call on a volunteer from one of the groups to summarize their list for the "CEO of Diocese" column. Write the suggestions on the board as they are told to you. Call on a volunteer from the next table group to add any qualification not mentioned. Repeat with representatives from each group and then continue the same process for the other three job descriptions. One or more of the job positions may have several of the following qualifications:

   Counselor

   Financial expertise

   Preaching skills

   Love for the Lord

   Teaching skills

   Knowledge of family issues

   Compassion for the grieving

   Forgiving

   Knowledge of theology

6. Next, ask the participants to read the introductions of Bishop Steven, Father Tony, Father Simeon, and Mr. Bambrick on pages 61-62. Ask them to match the name of the person with the job he is most qualified for in a particular column. Call on volunteers to suggest various possibilities. Then say:

> Go through each list on your own and put a check mark by any qualification that is held exclusively by an ordained minister and a star by any qualification that can be possessed by any person, ordained or not.

7. Allow a few minutes for marking. Then call on the participants to help you mark your lists on the board using the same code. Say:

> Most qualifications for the jobs we have described are held by many in the Catholic Christian community, not just the ordained. If this is so, you may wonder what makes a priest's role unique within a community. Why is ordained leadership necessary in the church? What was Jesus' role in establishing certain styles of

leadership? In Part I, we will look at the symbols of the sacrament of holy orders to help provide answers. In Part II, we will examine the history of the ordained ministry to understand more of its function and importance in the Catholic church.

Part I: Qualities of Servant Leadership

(about 50 minutes)

1. Continue with the participants seated with their table groups. Begin a presentation at the board based on the following script.

Script

2. To answer the question of why we need ordained leadership, it's important to have an understanding of the meaning of the word priest. The most important role of a priest in any religion is as a mediator (write **priest=mediator**) or "go between" between God and humankind. In Jesus' time, for example, only the Jewish high priest was permitted to enter the Temple's holy of holies as a representative of his people.

   Christians believe that Jesus is the high priest. St. Thomas Aquinas wrote: **"Only Christ is the true priest** (write), the others being only his ministers." The church also understands that through his role as high priest, Jesus has made a kingdom of priests among the baptized. According to the *Catechism of the Catholic Church:* "The faithful exercise their baptismal priesthood through their participation, each according to his own vocation, in Christ's mission as priest, prophet, and king" (#1546).

   Therefore, it is accurate to say that **we are all priests in the common priesthood of the faithful** (write). The common priesthood is conferred in baptism. Using our own talents and gifts, we participate in the one priesthood of Christ. Saint Paul described our tasks in his first letter to the Corinthians.

3. Call two volunteers before the groups to read 1 Corinthians 12:12-26 in three parts as follows:

   First reader: verses 12-13

   Second reader: verses 14-21

   First reader: verses 22-26

   After the scripture reading, continue from the script.

Script (continued)

4. Many of the qualities for the leadership roles that were listed in the Opening Activity are certainly shared by many members of the common priesthood. Yet, Christ also calls some people to a **ministerial priesthood** (write). The gospels record that Jesus chose and appointed twelve apostles as "ones sent" to share the good news. This was the beginning of an apostolic tradition in which the bishops are seen as the successors to the apostles. Priests are the bishop's "helpers." Jesus did not leave a blueprint for how leaders would function in the early Christian communities, but through his actions and teachings, he did leave a model for Christian leaders that is much different from one we usually associate

with leaders of large groups. Jesus' example of leadership focuses on humble service, not powerful authority.

Scripture Exercise

5. Pass out bibles to each table group. Read the directions for "Leadership Values" on page 63. Tell the groups to divide up the passages evenly and begin working. Allow about five minutes for the individuals to read and mark their sections of the chart. Then tell the groups to go around the table, offering a brief synopsis of the passage and the value for leadership that Jesus is teaching. Everyone should record all the values for the second column from the speakers' reports.

6. Summarize the exercise. Call on volunteers to share values for each passage. Record some of the responses on the board. For example:

Matthew 5:13-16	**share the gospel through good example**
Matthew 6:31-34	**trust God in all things**
Matthew 10:7	**heal physical and spiritual pains**
Matthew 18:15-21	**forgive others in Jesus' name**
Matthew 20:20-28	**rule as a servant of others**
Matthew 26:26-29	**celebrate the eucharist regularly**

7. After the exercise summary, say:

The leadership in the early church was codified and eventually known as the ministerial priesthood. The ministerial priesthood is at the service of the common priesthood and is conferred in the sacrament of holy orders. As was touched on in the Opening Activity, there are three levels of ordination: episcopacy (bishops), presbyterate (priests), and diaconate (deacons). According to any job description, the first priority for bishops, priests, and deacons is to build up the people of God through service to all.

Activity

8. Provide scrap paper, a bible, and any resources materials you have collected, to each table. Ask the participants to turn to pages 64-67, "Facts and Features of Holy Orders," and explain the procedure for the activity. Say:

In a few minutes, a guest speaker, <u>name of speaker</u>, will join us to offer his reflections and understanding of his own vocation to the ministerial priesthood. But before he begins his presentation, I would like you to surprise him with your own knowledge of ordained ministry as well as check his knowledge! Take some time on your own to read each entry on pages 64-67. When you are finished, work with your group to write at least five questions about ordained ministry or the sacrament of holy orders based on the information on these pages or from the other resources. Before he begins his talk, a representative from your group will present him with one or more of your questions.

9. Allow at least ten minutes for reading and formulation of questions.

Guest Speaker Presentation

7. Welcome the priest you have invited to share reflections on his ministry based on Resource 13, "Ordained Ministry Speaker Preparation Sheet." Ask him if he would also answer a few of the questions the participants have prepared. Then, call a representative from one group to pose one question. After it has been answered and verified, call on another group's representative, and so on. If there is more time available after the speaker's presentation, repeat the process with additional questions from the groups.

Break

(about 5 minutes)

Allow about five minutes for a stretch, drink of water, etc. Make final preparations of the prayer space. Tell the participants to meet in the area you have reserved for prayer after the break with their books and pens.

Prayer Experience: Ministers of Good News

(about 15 minutes)

Journal Activity

1. Play some soft background music as the participants enter the prayer space. Ask them to sit in alone spots, however in places where they can hear your directions. Tell them to turn to the journal activity on page 68, "Laborers for the Harvest." Read the directions aloud. Allow about ten minutes for writing. Then call all to sit in a circle around the candle and container of sand.

2. Read the passage from Matthew 9:35-38. After the reading lead a shared discussion on the reading using the questions from the journal activity (listed below).

Questions

- Name a non-ordained person who has shared the good news of Christianity in a way that has made an impression on you. What did the person say? What did the person do?
- How have you exercised a leadership of service in the church?
- When was a time that someone put you down because you shared your faith?
- Name an ordained church leader you respect. Why do you respect this person? What qualities make this person a good spiritual leader?
- Jesus may be calling you to spend your life sharing in his ministry as a priest, religious, or lay minister. How open are you to responding to such a call?

Intercessory Prayer

3. Give a seed to each participant. Place the container of soil in the center of the circle. Have each participant read or paraphrase the prayer they wrote for an ordained minister and plant their seed in the soil container. The response for each prayer is, "Hear us, Lord."
4. After everyone has shared their prayer, ask everyone to stand, join hands, and recite an Our Father.
5. Then, pray:

 Regardless of the type of priesthood we are called to, our common ministry is to share God's word far and wide so that it may sprout and grow among all people. Help us, Lord, to remember all who lead and serve the church by serving humankind. We ask this in your name. Amen.

6. In conclusion, play a recording or lead the singing of "Seed, Scattered and Sown" by Dan Felten.

Part II: Holy Orders Through Time: Events and Issues

(about 40 minutes)

1. Ask the participants to sit near the board with their books and pens. Give a presentation based on the following script, of key events and corresponding issues involving the church's hierarchical structure from apostolic to contemporary times. As you proceed, write on the board the key words from page 69-70, "Holy Orders Through Time." Ask the participants to follow along from their books.

Script

2. **Early Church** In the early church, the functions now assigned to priests were performed by several different people: apostles ("the traveling emissary"), prophets ("one who speaks the word of God") and teachers ("instructor of the faith"). As the church established residential communities in several areas, the need for structure and organization led to the appointment of men called bishops who served and administered individual communities. These were not dioceses; rather, they were simply one-parish towns. There was no designated presider at eucharist during this time. The head of the household in which the community gathered presided over the eucharist. (Pause. Allow about three minutes for the participants to think about and share with a partner their responses to the accompanying issues' questions for this section. Then continue with the presentation.)

 State Religion In the third through fifth centuries, the role of the presbyter was more clearly defined. Bishops were elected by the people, but they received the laying-on of hands from another bishop. Priests were ordained by bishops, with other priests joining in the laying on of hands. After Christianity was legalized in 313, the state gave special privileges to the people ordained for religious service. These people came to be called "clergy" and a gap was created between them and the laity. A view took hold that the clergy were people devoted to "higher things of the spirit," lay people to the "lower things of the flesh." Priests were ordained exclusively for service in a parish; in fact, the ordination of anyone not called to serve in a particular parish was considered void. Bishops and priests were paid salaries by the state. (Pause. Allow about three minutes for the participants to think about and share their responses with a partner to the accompanying issues' questions for this section. Then continue with the presentation.)

Middle Ages Priests were involved in the feudal system of the times; they performed not only the sacramental functions but were also called on to collect taxes. They pledged loyalty to a feudal lord, not the bishop. Candidates for priesthood received little or no education and preparation prior to ordination. Another dynamic influencing the priesthood of the time was monasticism. The life of the monk was marked by separation from the world for the purposes of prayer, study, and strict discipline. A promise of celibacy was taken as a public sign of their dedication and separation from the world. By the twelfth century, celibacy had become a universal requirement for priests of the Roman church. Prior to this time, married priests were permitted. (Pause. Allow about three minutes for the participants to think about and share with a partner their responses to the accompanying issues' questions for this section. Then continue with the presentation.)

Reformation and Trent Martin Luther, a Catholic priest and monk, was the most prominent of the reformers. The reformers emphasized the common priesthood of all believers and said that there was no special ministerial power received through the sacrament of holy orders. The Council of Trent countered this argument by defining holy orders as one of the seven sacraments and stating that bishops, priests, and deacons do not depend on a call of the community for their authority and powers. The Council of Trent inspired reform in the church, including the establishment of seminaries for assisting the preparation of candidates to the priesthood. (Pause. Allow about three minutes for the participants to think about and share with a partner their responses to the accompanying issues' questions for this section. Then continue with the presentation.)

Vatican II and Beyond The documents of the Second Vatican Council reaffirm the common priesthood of the baptized, that all the baptized participate in some way in the priesthood and mission of Christ. The Council describes priesthood in terms of servant leadership and says that priests cannot be of service to others if they remain strangers to the life and conditions of those around them. As good shepherds, priests are called to know their sheep. The bishop with the priest serve the faithful by preaching the gospel, leading public worship, and seeing that the mission of Jesus is carried out. Although the bishop and priest are called to serve all of humankind, special attention must be given to the poor and the lowly to whom they have been entrusted in a special way. The permanent diaconate is re-established.

Public Interview

3. Allow about three minutes for the participants to think about and share their responses to the final question. Then, use the public interview method of dialoguing (see Appendix, page 121) to summarize the presentation. Call one person to the front of the group and use the related issues' questions from the Participant

Book as a basis for the discussion. Supplement with questions of your own and those listed below. As time allows, call more participants to be interviewed in front of the group.

Questions

- What do you consider to be a priest's primary function?
- Tell about a time a priest comforted you or a family member in a time of sadness.
- Tell about an occasion when a priest shared a joyful occasion with you and your family.
- What are three things you know about your local bishop?
- What do you think would be missing in parishes without priests, besides someone to lead sacraments?
- The pope has said that the issue of women being priests is closed for debate. How do you feel about this?
- Finish this sentence: One thing that attracts me to the lifestyle of a priest is . . .
- What's the best advice you ever received from a priest?
- How do you envision the ordained ministry one hundred years from now?

Conclusion

(about 5 minutes)

Attendance/Meeting Verification

1. Ask the groups to report to tables with their group moderators who will take attendance and check their summaries and mentor signatures from Teen-Mentor Meeting 6.

Mentor Meeting Reminder

2. Preview Teen-Mentor Meeting 7 (pages 71-72 in the Participant Book). Offer specific directions as needed. For each participant who is interested in doing the letter-writing to a diocesan or religious community vocation director, provide a name and address. Tell them to record this information in the Mentor Memo panels.
3. Remind the participants of the date of Session Eight. Dismiss them on time.

Session Eight

Marriage: A Living Sacrament

Objectives

The purpose of this session is to help the participants:

- uncover key symbols for married life in the rite of matrimony;
- understand that intimate sharing between a husband and wife is a means of growing in God's grace;
- discover how the rhythm of family life parallels the rhythm celebrated by the faith community through the seven sacraments.

Overview

The sacrament of matrimony, like holy orders, is a sacrament at the service of the communion (*CCC*, #1533). It is a covenant relationship between a man and woman to live their vocation of love and service to God, to one another, and to the Christian community. Matrimony calls a couple to help each other grow in holiness, facing life together with openness to where God leads them. It also calls the couple to be a living sign of God's love through the way they live; in their everyday relationship, in their sexual union, and in their willingness to share their love by bringing life to others, especially in the welcoming of children. In Part I of this session, the participants examine the symbols of the rite of matrimony, including the couple themselves, the rings that are exchanged, the word of God that is shared, the vows that are spoken, and the community of friends and family that are present. The Prayer Experience is a scripture reflection that typifies the esteem God and God's People have had for the covenant relationship of marriage. In Part II, through the sharing of a guest panel of married couples, the participants witness how the seven sacraments parallel the life experiences of families.

Session Eight

Mentor Component

The teens and mentors meet for the final time at this session. Time is reserved in the final twenty minutes of this session for the mentors and teens to conduct Teen-Mentor Meeting 8. It is recommended that you invite the mentors to the entire session. (A second option is to ask the mentors to arrive at the break time just prior to the start of the Prayer Experience.) You may also consider inviting one or more mentors and spouses to form the panel on marriage and family life (see Special Preparations).

Session Outline

Opening Activity: Good Answer! Good Answer! (about 20 minutes)
Part I: The Symbols of Holy Matrimony (about 50 minutes)
Break (about 5 minutes)
Prayer Experience: Scripture Reflection on Marriage (about 25 minutes)
Part II: The Church of the Home (about 30 minutes)
Mentor Meeting, Feedback and Conclusion (about 20 minutes)

Supplies

For this session you will need:

- pens and pencils
- extra copies of the Participant Book
- two pieces of letter-writing paper
- two letter-size envelopes
- two school backpacks with zippers
- highlight markers (one for every two participants)
- copies of Resource 14, "Scripture Prayer" (one for each participant)
- scissors
- bibles
- a recording of quiet background music
- tape or CD player
- copies of Resource 15, "Marriage Panel Preparation Sheet"

Special Preparations

1. Cut apart the scripture passages on Resource 14 and assemble them in packets so that each participant will receive one complete set.
2. Arrange for a panel of married couples to speak to the teens about marriage and family life based on the outline on Resource 15, "Marriage Panel Preparation Sheet." A panel with three couples of a wide variety of ages and lengths

of marriage serves well. If possible, use mentors and their spouses to serve in this capacity.

3. Adapt the teen-mentor meeting portion of the session to the special character of your course. Invite the mentors as far in advance as possible. For any participants whose mentors can't be present, invite a parent or other significant adult to be with them at this occasion. Specify the time for arrival.
4. Invite two or three teens to share brief reflections on the teen-mentor experience (see Mentor Meeting, Feedback and Conclusion, No. 2).

Settings

You will need the following areas for this session:

1. A large area where adults and teens can gather in a relaxed and comfortable atmosphere with viewing access to the board.
2. An area where teens (and mentors) can gather around circular or square tables in groups of six to eight.
3. "Alone" spots—places where the teens (and mentors) can be at least six feet away from each other.
4. An area for the Prayer Experience. Plan to arrange the large group meeting area into a comfortable setting for the closing prayer portion of the Prayer Experience.

Opening Activity:
Good Answer! Good Answer!

(about 20 minutes)

Welcome/Check-in

1. Greet the participants as they arrive and have them check in with their group moderators and show their Teen-Mentor Meeting 7 summary pages and mentor's verification signatures.

Survey Game

2. Call everyone to the large meeting space and divide the participants into two sides for a game based on the television program *Family Feud*. Remind the participants of the rules of the game and adaptations as follows:

Game Rules

- One representative from each team comes forward.
- A question (see page 109) involving weddings, marriage, and family life is read.

- The first representative to "buzz-in" (make a buzzing sound) gets to answer first. If the given answer is the number-one surveyed answer from a designated group, his or her team (e.g., team "A") controls the board. (If not, the representative from team B tries to guess a higher surveyed item.)
- The members of the team (e.g., team A) work together to guess the remainder of the surveyed answers. Two incorrect answers gives control to team B. Team B works together to guess any remaining answer. After the entire category is solved or two strikes for Team B, the round ends. Scoring is determined as follows:

  Number-one surveyed answer=5 points

  Number-two surveyed answer=4 points

  Number-three surveyed answer=3 points

  Number-four surveyed answer=2 points

  Number-five surveyed answer=1 point

3. Say:

   We surveyed twenty fourth-graders in Santa Monica, California about things involving weddings, marriage, and family life. Can I have a representative from each team for round 1?

4. Begin play for round 1. Continue with new team representatives to begin rounds 2 to 5. Use the questions and results of the fourth-grade survey below. The numbers in parenthesis indicate the number of fourth-graders who gave that answer.

Round 1

Q: What's the best part of a wedding reception?

1. Cake (10)
2. The meal (4)
3. Dancing (3)
4. Music (2)
5. Seeing my cousins (1)

Round 2

Q: What age do most people get married?

1. 25 (8)
2. 21 (5)
3. 30 (4)
4. 18 (2)
5. 28 (1)

Round 3

Q: What do married people do when they go out for the evening together without the kids?

1. Go to movies (7)
2. Go to dinner (6)
3. Go shopping (4)
4. Go to games (2)
5. Visit friends (1)

Round 4

Q: What do married people argue about?

1. Problems with the kids (6)
2. Money (5)
3. Messy house (5)
4. What's for supper (3)
5. What to watch on television (1)

Round 5

Q: Who's in a wedding besides the bride and groom?

1. The best man (6)
2. The bride's best friend/maid of honor (5)
3. The ring bearer (4)
4. The priest (3)
5. The bride/groom's parents (2)

5. Keep a running score after each round. Determine a winning team after five rounds. Reward the winners with a round of applause.

   Optional: Develop questions of your own about weddings, marriage, and/or family life and survey a "control group" to determine the five most popular responses. Use the new questions to extend the game.

Part I: The Symbols of Holy Matrimony

(about 50 minutes)

1. Have the participants sit near the board with their books and a pens. Choose three volunteers to take part in a demonstration. Place the two sheets of letter quality paper, two envelopes, and two backpacks on an opposite side of the room. Tell two of the volunteers they will work together as a team. The remaining volunteer will work alone. Give the following directions. Say, for example:

   I am going to give you some instructions for a race. The team members, Bob and Kathy, work together. Steve works alone. When I say "go" race to the other side of the room. On your piece of paper, print the words "It is not good for a person to be alone." Seal the paper in an envelope, put the envelope in the backpack, zip the backpack and race back to this spot. By the way, you can only use your non-writing hand for the entire activity. Place your writing hands behind your backs. Ready? Go!

2. After the race, say:

   As you witnessed, some things are better done with the help of another. The authors of the book of Genesis (2:18), in reflecting on the human need for relationship, wrote: **"It is not good for a person to be alone"** (write). We are created to be in relationship with one another, as co-workers for building God's reign. This session explores a special kind of relationship that reveals God's love, the relationship of marriage.

3. Read or summarize the opening text on page 73. Print a heading on the board, **The Symbols of Holy Matrimony**. Then, continue with a presentation from the following script. As you list each symbol on the board, have the participants write the names near the sketches or photos of the symbols on page 74 of the Participant Book.

Script

4. What does it mean to say that the couple is the main symbol of the sacrament of matrimony? (Write: **couple=main symbol**) Through the many stages of forming and developing a relationship, the man and woman make a decision that their mutual vocation, or "call to holiness," is to continue to nurture their relationship and grow in love for one another. They understand that the promises they make to one another in the sacrament of matrimony are a covenant. Like God's covenant with the Chosen People and Jesus' covenant with the church, their marriage covenant is permanent and unbreakable.

   Certainly, it's a thought-filled and busy road for a couple just to reach their wedding day. Nowadays, it is the man and woman themselves who initiate the process. Physical attraction, common interests, and compatible personalities are among the things that first bring a couple together. Sometimes this initial experience is called "falling in love," but it evolves to more than superficial attraction as the relationship develops. Gradually, during a period traditionally known as courtship, the couple grows in trust and commitment for one another.

   The couple is the main symbol of the sacrament of matrimony because they are the ministers of the sacrament. Through the taking of vows, or promises, the couple makes a public pledge of their love and commitment for one another. This promise of consent is the main part of the rite of marriage. These vows are spoken in a church and witnessed by family and friends. The official witness of the sacrament representing the church is a priest or deacon. **Vows** and the **community of faith** are two other symbols of matrimony.

   A Catholic wedding normally takes place during the Mass because of the connection of all the sacraments to the life, death, and resurrection of Jesus. *The Catechism of the Catholic Church* states: "It is therefore fitting that the spouses should seal their consent to give themselves to each other through the offering of Christ for his Church made present in the Eucharistic sacrifice . . ." (#1621).

   As part of the Mass, the readings for the **liturgy of the word** are chosen, often by the couple themselves, to speak especially to the theme of married love. After the exchange of rings, the priest or deacon extends his hands and offers a **nuptial blessing** for the couple, a sharing of God's grace for courage, strength, perseverance, and love in their lives together.

   A customary but optional symbol of holy matrimony is the ring. By its shape, the **ring** is a symbol of eternal love. It is a reminder to the husband of wife of their love for one another when they are separated. The ring is also a sign of fidelity, or faithfulness, between a husband and wife. In marriage, the book of Genesis tells us, a man and woman "become one flesh" (Gn 2:24). Sexual intercourse between a wife and a husband is a special sign of this communion of two persons with God. In marriage, sexual intercourse is a means of growing closer to each other and to God. Just as a person is holier after receiving communion or the sacrament of reconciliation, the husband and wife are holier, closer to God, after giving themselves in love to the marriage partner. This sexual sharing is intended to provide both a *unitive* dimension, bringing a husband and wife closer together in loving friendship, and a *procreative* dimension, cooperating with God in being open to accepting a child as a result of their union.

5. To summarize and offer more information on these symbols, read or have the participants individually read the text under "Matrimonial Consent" on page 75.

Then, point out the drawing of the ring on page 74. Ask the participants to write words or phrases in the center of the ring to describe the kinds of qualities they would be looking for in a marriage partner. Allow a few minutes. Then ask them to form quickly into groups of four to six and go around the group sharing one quality that is most important for them. If there is time, tell them to go around a second and third time sharing other qualities.

6. Title a second category on the board, **Qualities of a Marriage Partner**, and call on representatives from each group to list several of their group's responses. Record them on the board. Add any qualities from the list of example, below, that are not mentioned.

Examples

- forgiving
- warm and caring
- attractive
- sense of humor
- good with children
- prayerful
- holy
- committed

Inventory Sharing

7. Say:

> At some point, a couple preparing for marriage considers the implications of making a life-long commitment in marriage. This often means taking inventory on key issues in their personal lives and considering their compatibility to one another. The church sponsors such inventories as part of a preparation program for the sacrament of matrimony. A sample inventory is on page 76. Fill in the chart on your own. Then wait for further direction.

Allow five to ten minutes for marking. Then pair the participants with a person of the opposite sex. Have the boys and girls line up in separate lines, shortest to tallest. Pair the first two of each line, the next two, etc. (If there is an unequal distribution, use adult moderators to make a pair or form some groups with three people.) Pass out a highlight marker to each pair. Ask them to share their responses to each question and the reasons for marking as they did. Say:

> Use the highlight marker to outline the squares of any responses you agree on.

8. Allow ten minutes for discussion. Then ask all the participants to stand near the person they were paired with. Say:

> If you had only one square highlighted, be seated. (Pause.) If you had two squares highlighted, be seated.

Continue in this manner until you designate the pairs with the most common responses. Call one of these pairs to sit in two chairs facing the group. Dialogue with them on their responses to the inventory. Allow each person a chance to address each of the following questions. Also add some questions of your own.

Questions

- Which issue do you consider most important? Why?
- Which issue to you consider least important? Why?
- Which issue(s) would you insist on agreement between you and a potential spouse before you would consider marriage?
- What steps could be taken to resolve a disagreement involving the issue in number one (for example)?

Choose another pair to sit in the chairs and dialogue. (You may choose a pair that had the least agreement among answers.) Continue with other pairs as time allows.

Break

(about 5 minutes)

Allow a brief time for a stretch, drink of water, etc. Tell the participants to gather in the large meeting area after the break. Plan to greet the guest speakers and mentors if they are arriving at this time.

Prayer Experience: Scripture Reflection on Marriage

(about 25 minutes)

1. Give everyone a bible and a set of the "Scripture Prayer" starters. Say:

   Work together to find these ten passages in the Gospels. Use the prayer starters as bookmarks. Don't read the passages yet.

   When all the bibles are marked, say:

   Now take your bibles and move to a place in this room where you can be alone. Make sure you are at least six feet from anyone else and not anywhere near someone who may bother you.

   When all are settled and quiet, give a talk based on the following prayer script.

Prayer Script

2. Our history and tradition tell us that Jesus was never married. Nor did he leave us with any words instituting marriage as a sacrament. But Jesus certainly left many examples of

his support for married love, for the dignity of women, and the for the indissolubility of marriage.

Jesus taught the meaning of marriage as it was intended from the beginning of time, that God intends for man and woman to come together to form an unbreakable union. In Moses' day, the people had argued about marriage and were granted a law covering divorce. Jesus refuted the law, saying "what God has joined, no person must separate" (Mt 19:6).

Jesus' very first miracle took place at a wedding. At the request of his mother, he changed water to wine. The very fact that Jesus attended a wedding celebration shows that he supported the commitment of married love.

One of the images for the church is the "Bride of Christ." This means that Jesus loves and is committed to us, the faithful members of this community, as his bride. His love for his people is the model for all loving and committed relationships.

We are going to try to experience more about Jesus' words and actions concerning love and marriage. When I finish giving the directions, turn to any passage you have marked. Read the passage several times, prayerfully and attentively. Spend some time talking to Jesus about the passage, asking him to tell you what message he wants you to hear in those words. Write his message to you on the marker, and then turn to another passage. It isn't necessary to do all ten passages. Spend as much time as you can talking with Jesus about any of them.

Quiet your heart now. Ask Jesus to speak to you through the words of his gospel. When your heart is ready, open the bible and begin.

3. Play some quiet music as a background to the scripture prayer. Allow fifteen to twenty minutes, depending on the prayerfulness of the group.

4. Ask the participants to gather in groups of four to six. Say:

Take turns sharing your favorite passage. Explain to your group what personal message those words of scripture held for you today.

Part II: The Church of the Home

(about 30 minutes)

1. Move to the large meeting area. Tell the participants that they are going to hear from a panel of married couples on some of the issues and experiences involved in a sacramental marriage. Ask them to begin to think about one question on marriage they may wish to address to the panel.

Panel Presentation on Marriage

2. Set up a panel (see Appendix, page 121) of chairs facing the group. Welcome the married couples. Use the following format as suggested on Resource 15, "Marriage Panel Preparation Sheet": (1) each couple introduces themselves and provides a brief history of their marriage; (2) each couple shares a brief reflection

based on one of the marriage issues listed on the resource sheet; (3) the participants address questions on marriage to the panel members. (You may also ask the panel members to respond to the questions listed on Resource 15.)

3. After the panel presentation, allow about five minutes for summary. Say:

   The celebration of the sacrament of matrimony is only the beginning of Christian marriage. As with the other sacraments, the celebration marks us publicly and strengthens us in God's grace as we begin the task of living the sacrament. For example, the Second Vatican Council called the family the domestic church or the church of the home. In marriage, the husband and wife are a living sign or sacrament of God's love in the lives of their children. In turn, the children are living signs of God's love to their parents. Let's examine some of the rhythms of family life and how they parallel the signs and actions of the seven sacraments.

4. Create the following chart on the board. Go over each of the parallel signs of family and parish life as the participants follow along on page 77 of their books. Call on volunteers to suggest the sacraments that go in column two. Have them write their names in their books as listed below.

The Church of the Home	The Church of the Parish
Welcomes and initiates new members to the family (customs, rules, traditions)	Baptism Confirmation
Shares meals of unity	Eucharist
Fights and forgives	Reconciliation
Heals and comforts one another	Anointing of the Sick
Encourages its members to service and leadership	Holy Orders
Nurtures life-giving relationships	Matrimony

Mentor Meeting, Feedback and Conclusion

(about 20 minutes)

Introduction of Mentors

1. Ask the group to assemble close to you, the teens sitting next to their mentors. Ask each teen one at a time to stand and formally introduce his or her mentor. (If the group is too large or time is short, you may simply welcome and introduce the mentors to all.)

2. Invite two or three teens to share general reflections about the mentor relationship. (These speakers should be invited and prepared in advance of the session.) The reflections might include some or all of the following points:

- words of advice offered by the mentor that the teen will always remember
- appreciation for the time the mentor spent meeting with you
- a personal insight on the meaningful nature of the teen-mentor relationship

Also allow opportunity for any mentors who wish to share with the group to do so. Conclude the talks with a round of applause for all the mentors.

Teen-Mentor Meeting 8

3. Direct the teen-mentor pairs to move to separate areas of the room to conduct Teen-Mentor Meeting 8 from pages 78-79 of the Participant Book.
4. Allow about ten minutes for the teen-mentor meeting. Then call everyone together. As time allows, ask teens and mentors to share the responses for the columns of the chart on page 77.
5. Remind the teens and adults of other events in your program. Thank them for their attendance and participation and bid them farewell.

Appendix

Eight Be-Attitudes for Session Directors

1. Be prepared.

Study the manual carefully. Think through the session plans, outline them, and prepare your own note cards for teaching them. Visualize each activity in your mind, "seeing" it step by step. You should clearly understand the purpose and expected outcome.

2. Be yourself.

Make the material your own. Think about it; pray about it; if possible, talk about it with other adults. Use the ideas in the manual creatively—add your own examples, substitute other activities, shorten or lengthen sections. The sessions should come across to the participants as *yours*, not as the book's.

3. Be organized.

Have a definite plan of action for each part of a session. Be especially clear about giving directions for discussion exercises and activities. Have all the materials ready for quick distribution.

4. Be flexible.

Be ready to adjust your well-organized plan at a moment's notice. Some activities may last longer or shorter than expected; some won't fit the mood of the evening; some won't work for you or your group. Always have more material planned than you think you will need. Keep your eye on the clock; if you're running short of time, shorten or drop something—but, please, not the Prayer Experience!

5. Be open.

Listen to what the young people have to say, and encourage them to listen to one another. Accept their feelings and ideas even if you don't agree with them. Be ready at times to challenge them (always respectfully) on ideas and positions that are inconsistent, erroneous, or unclear.

6. Be firm.

Do not allow the candidates to be disrespectful of you or to one another. Maintain an orderly, controlled atmosphere even during fun times. Let the young people know that you expect adult conduct from them. (All of this will be made much easier by the presence of adult participants in the group.)

7. Be happy.

Enjoy the young people. Enjoy their nonsense and exuberance as well as their thoughtfulness and serious sharing. Let them know that you like being with them.

8. Be-lieve.

Believe that you aren't in this business alone, that God and the Christian community play active roles in the process of transmitting and sharing faith. Believe that God is involved in the lives of your young people, that the action of God's grace precedes, accompanies, and follows all your efforts. Believe that the faith is alive in your parish community, and that the whole parish is helping in some way to transmit that faith to its youth.

Dialogue: Why and How

The *Developing Faith* series depends for its effectiveness on the interaction of the participants—the interaction of teens with adults, and of teens with teens. This interaction is brought about primarily through *dialogue*. Some of the dialogue in the program is light, fun, humorous. Its purpose is to break down barriers and to build mutual understanding and enjoyment. It also makes serious dialogue possible—serious dialogue in which the teens share with one another their dreams and hopes, their questions and doubts, their values and goals, their faith and prayer.

The dialogue technique is based on several assumptions:

- that faith is an already-present reality in each person, and that dialogue helps to surface, affirm, and strengthen that faith;
- that each person is a source of truth and wisdom, and that the truth of each individual is meant for and needed by the entire community;
- that all people, but especially youth, want to open their hearts and share their deepest beliefs and doubts—all they need is listeners who care;
- that talking about the deepest values in one's life helps to clarify and strengthen them for the speaker, that one understands better what one has just tried to explain to another;
- that the faith of the listener is also strengthened by the dialogue process; one of the most powerful ways of alerting a person to the action of God in his or her life is to hear about God's action in the life of another;
- that dialogue creates the common meaning system that enables those who participate in honest dialogue to become a community.

Dialogue of the sort described here can happen only in an atmosphere of openness and trust. To establish such an atmosphere is to a large extent the responsibility of the session director. But it is also true that the dialogue itself creates the atmosphere. Young people learn to share deeply with one another and with adults by doing it. The director's role is to make the doing easy.

Dialoguing Principles

The dialogue activities in this mini-course are designed to encourage sharing. Though each activity uses a slightly different dialogue technique, some general methodological principles apply to all of them:

Pre-response

Give everyone a chance to record his or her response in some way before asking any individual to respond orally. The pre-response might be written, drawn, shown with hand signals, or indicated by body positions. Make the pre-response easy by asking a very specific question with a concrete answer, by providing a sentence starter to be completed, by giving a spread of answers to choose from. This technique gets everyone involved in answering the question, makes it clear that there is a spread of opinion on the answer rather than the one "right" response, and creates the need for an individual to examine a position contrary to other ideas being presented.

Dialogue starter

Make it easy to get the dialogue started by designating the first speaker, often in a humorous way; for example, the person with the curliest hair, the person with the next birthday, the person wearing the baggiest pants. Each person will then take a turn around the circle. The starter designation usually creates a burst of laughter, thus further relaxing the group.

Pass option

Tell the group that the sharing must always be done freely. If at any time a participant is asked a question he or she doesn't know how to answer, or does not want to answer in public, the person simply says "Pass." If participants choose to respond, however, their answers should be as honest as possible. The pass option is, perhaps, the single most powerful technique in creating an atmosphere where open dialogue can happen. Given the choice of either answering honestly or passing, young people almost always choose to answer. But the pass is always there as a safe and easy way out when things get too hot to handle. It is imperative that the pass option be respected by the directors and by all participants.

Gradual deepening

Move the dialogue gradually from light, easy topics to more serious ones. The easier sharing teaches the technique and warms the participants, thus facilitating deeper sharing.

Listening

Help your group see the important role of the *listener* in the dialogue process. A person is encouraged to share by sensing that someone is really listening. Everyone in the dialogue circle shares in the listening role. It is important for all the members of the group to look at the speaker, to respond facially to what is said, and to ask follow-up questions. The adults should be especially present to each speaker; at the same time the adults will need to be careful not to become the focus toward which all answers are directed.

Dialoguing Activities

Activities which feature dialogue as a central component include the following:

One-on-one

Designate some way for the participants to pair off (for example, choose as a partner someone you haven't talked to this week, choose a partner who is a different generation or sex, choose a partner who was born in the same month as you). Give the participants something specific to think about and allow a moment of thinking time (for example, think about a living person you admire, think about something you consider evil, think about a recent time you knew God was helping you). Designate which partner should share first. Switch partners and repeat with a new topic.

Panel

Select about six participants to be on a panel. Ways of selecting the panel include asking for volunteers, having each circle select its "least shy" person, drawing names from a hat, calling on elected officers, and so on. Dialogue with the panelists in front of the group for twenty minutes or so. Work from a prepared set of questions but be open to the movement of the dialogue. Listen carefully to the responses and ask follow-up questions based on them. Encourage the panelists to respond to one another. Also encourage response and questions from the audience. You may wish to select a second group of panelists half-way through the session. (This method is a good way for the director to demonstrate the dialogue technique for other participating adults.)

Public interview

Ask for a volunteer who would be willing to dialogue with you in front of the entire group. Interview the person about some area of life that is important to him or her. Work from prepared questions but be flexible.

On the spot

Have the participants write their names on small cards. Collect the cards and shuffle them conspicuously. Pick one name from the pack and ask the person picked if he or she is willing to be "on the spot" for a few minutes. If so, ask a few dialogue questions, then pick another name. The person picked may pass altogether, or pass on any question asked. You may want to keep a set of name cards handy so that you can use this technique at a moment's notice.

Chain reaction

Call on one person to share his or her pre-response to a question. Dialogue briefly with the person about the response, then tell the person to select the next responder. Designate in some way who can be picked; for example, you must pick a person from a different group, a person of the opposite sex.

Grouping Tips

You will need some fast, efficient ways of dividing the participants into dialogue circles. The composition of these circles is important for the success of each session. Each group should contain an even distribution of group moderators, visiting adults, males and females, outspoken and shy persons, and so forth. Try as much as possible to separate members of friendship groups, and always separate family members. It is usually better not to allow participants to select their own groups. Some grouping methods are listed in each of the sessions as required. Some other grouping methods are listed below:

Name tags

If you know ahead of time who will be attending the session, you can use the name tags to designate groups. Follow these steps:

1. Before the session make a name tag for each participant, youth and adult.
2. Put the name tags in groups of eight, selecting the kind of distribution you want in each group.
3. Put a group symbol (letter, number, sign) on each name tag in the pack.
4. Put all the tags back in alphabetical order so they will be easy for the participants to pick up.
5. Put a corresponding group symbol at each table. As participants arrive, ask them to find their symbol and sit at that table.

Leadership distribution

Use this method to establish groupings that will last for several sessions or for the entire program. Note that this method takes a while. The grouping itself should not be done during class time, nor in the presence of the group.

In class

1. Give everyone, adults and youth, three small tally slips (papers about 1" x 2").
2. Ask each person to select three young people in the class who have leadership qualities. Write one name on each paper and fold once. (If the group is large, you may wish to hand out lists with all the names.)
3. Collect the votes.

Privately

1. Put the votes in piles: all John's votes in one pile, Mary's in another, and so forth. Count the votes.
2. Decide how many groups you will need. If you need seven, for example, select the seven people with the most votes. Put one in each group and name him or her the *youth leader* of the group. Select the next seven

people with the most votes and name them *co-leaders*. If the leader is a boy, try to have the co-leader be a girl. Continue to distribute the names according to the votes received. Work for a balance of boys and girls.

3. Assign a group moderator for each group.
4. List all the names for future reference. Put the names of the youth leader and co-leader at the top of the list, but arrange the other names alphabetically so that the persons receiving the least votes will not appear last.

Make use of the leaders in various ways throughout the program. Give them responsibility in planning, making decisions, and so on.

Friendship-group distribution

Use this method if you want to establish grouping for a longer session such as a retreat, or for several sessions. It will also work for one session.

1. As the participants arrive, invite them to sit at tables wherever they choose. They will sit with their natural friendship groups.
2. Give out small cards, one to each person, and ask everyone to write first and last names on the card.
3. Collect the cards yourself, being careful to keep together the cards of people who are sitting together.
4. Decide how many groups you will need (for example, seven). Deal the cards into seven piles as follows. Begin with adults. Then distribute the cards of the boys; then of the girls. The people who were sitting together will automatically end up in different groups.

Parallel lines

This is a fast, easy method for dividing up a very large group, especially if you have no way of knowing beforehand how many people to expect.

1. Estimate the highest number of participants you could logically expect for the session (for example, 160). Divide that number by eight to determine how many groups you might have (for example, twenty). Set up circles of chairs with eight chairs in each. Number the circles from one to twenty.
2. As the participants arrive, have them sign in, adults on one paper, youth on another. Number the papers for easy counting.
3. When all have assembled, check the sign-in sheets to see the total number present and divide by eight to determine how many groups you will actually need. (If it's more than twenty, run for more chairs!)
4. Determine what kind of distribution you want in each group; for example, men, women, boys, girls. Ask the participants to form four parallel lines: men, women, boys, girls.
5. Stand in front of the four lines. Skim off the first four across and send them to circle one; send the second four to circle two; the next four to circle three; and so on until you reach the total number of circles that you need. Half-way down the lines you will begin again with circle one.

6. As you near the end, the lines will be uneven. Fill in the shorter lines from the longer ones.
7. Check to see if any group contains two members of one family. If so, ask one of the family members to switch places with someone of the same age and sex in another group.

Count off

This is the old standby for grouping. Its disadvantage is that some young people will conveniently "forget" their number and move to a circle of their choice rather than to the one assigned.

1. Decide how many groups you will need (for example, seven).
2. Go down the row (or around the circle) and ask each person to count off from one to seven. Count off the group moderators first, then the visiting adults, then the youth.
3. Move to the circles one group at a time. Say, for example: "All the one's follow Mr. Jones, all the two's Mrs. Smith, etc. (Moving to one group at a time makes it more difficult for a person to "forget" and go to the wrong group.)

Free choice method

Once in a while allow the participants to choose their own groups. Do this especially for shorter discussion activities of a more personal nature. This works well when the groupings are just two or three people also.

Tear-out Resource Section

Multiple copies of the following pages are needed for the *Sacraments: A Way of Life* sessions (see the individual sessions for specific instructions on the use of the materials). The pages are perforated for your convenience in copying the materials for distribution during the sessions.

Mentor Interview and Registration Form

Name: ______________________________

Address: ______________________________

____

Day Telephone: ______________ Night Telephone: ______________

Teen's Name: ______________________________

Relationship: ______________________________

Comments: ______________________________

____

____

____

____

____

____

____

____

____

____

Interviewed by: ______________________________

Date: ______________________________

Resource 1

Class Yearbook Tally Sheet

Directions: Record after each "profession" the photo numbers ascribed by the people at your table.

Peacemaker ____

President ____

Rock Star ____

Model ____

Banker ____

Weight-lifter ____

Parent of Eight Children ____

Stand-up Comic ____

Felon ____

Gourmet Chef ____

Dentist ____

Resource 2

Group Initiation Chart

Medical Doctors

Personal Qualities	*Apprenticeship*	*Special Rituals*	*After Acceptance*
intelligence, drive, endurance, compassion	medical school internship/residency rotations to different areas of medicine; cannot yet prescribe medicine	graduations, title of "doctor" given after graduation, ceremonies after residency, Hippocratic oath	prescribe medicine and practice with minimum supervision; still is expected to continue learning and maintain regular contact with other doctors

Professional Athletes

Personal Qualities	*Apprenticeship*	*Special Rituals*	*After Acceptance*
physical fitness, self-discipline, patience	rookie status; minor league or college training; second-string status; observes experienced players	player drafts, use of uniform with assigned number and name, photo on sport's card	is expected to know how to play well; helps out new players; develops own unique style; continues to improve

Military Officers

Personal Qualities	*Apprenticeship*	*Special Rituals*	*After Acceptance*
self-discipline, leadership ability, perseverance, loyalty	basic training which includes learning the rules, chain of command, skills, more responsibility and privileges for each rank, etc.	moving up ranks different clothing and "stripes," salutes oaths to defend country	has responsibility for others; is able to make decisions, helps new recruits, keeps abreast of what is going on, maintains regular contact with other officers

American Citizens

Personal Qualities	*Apprenticeship*	*Special Rituals*	*After Acceptance*
willingness to learn, to participate in the community, tolerance of pluralism	learn the language and culture; live in the U.S. for a certain amount of time; limited privileges; supervised by immigration department	show a desire and commitment to take on citizenship responsibilities—take an oath of allegiance, receive a certificate and flag	able to vote, pay taxes, and contribute positively to the life of the people; has privileges and responsibilities of full citizen

College Fraternity/Sorority

Personal Qualities	*Apprenticeship*	*Special Rituals*	*After Acceptance*
loyalty, commitment, service-oriented	live with the group; learn the group's way of life; serve the initiated members; you are called "pledge"	"hazing"—to test commitment to the group; pin or ring ceremony to mark acceptance; can live in frat/sorority house house	has all privileges of full membership; expected to follow group's code; can initiate new members; has a network of connections at other colleges

Resource 3

Church Initiation Chart

Catholic Christian

Personal Qualities	*Apprenticeship*	*Special Rituals*	*After Acceptance*
willingness to serve, love others	building relationships with others	wearing white garment	sharing eucharist weekly
openness to trust God	telling personal life and faith stories	water immersion or pouring	witnessing to gospel values
willingness to take part in church life	learning the stories, traditions and beliefs of the community	making pledge/ promises	using gifts and talents for the reign of God
faith, prayer	involvment in service and discipleship	anointings	participating in ministry of church
		accepting lighted candle	continuing to grow in faith and knowledge
		sharing bread and wine	expanding prayer life

Resource 4

Christian Initiation Speaker Preparation Sheet

Thank you for agreeing to speak with the teenagers in a sacrament mini-course about your experience in the adult Christian initiation process. Please plan to talk for approximately ten minutes. There will be a brief question and answer period to follow. Try to include the following points in your presentation.

- What was your role in the initiation process (catechumen, sponsor, team member)?

- What were some common reasons catechumens gave for their initial attraction to the Catholic church?

- Tell about some of the various steps of the initiation process (faith-sharing, service, liturgy of the word).

- What requirement of the Catholic faith did you or others see as most difficult?

- Tell about the liturgical rituals that were a part of the initiation process.

- Explain how the sacraments of initiation—baptism, confirmation, and eucharist—were incorporated into the Easter vigil liturgy.

Resource 5

Walking Through the Rituals of Initiation

Reader 1: We become the people of God as we pass through water. The Hebrews passed through the waters of the Red Sea as they journeyed to freedom. When Jesus was baptized in the Jordan River, the sky opened and the Spirit, like a dove, descended upon him. A voice from the heavens said: "You are my beloved One; with you I am well pleased." We, too, are God's beloved chosen ones, called by name in baptism to be a sign of God's love to the world.

Reader 2: Through the waters of baptism, we have been filled with new life. Bless us, God, and keep us united in Jesus' name.

Reader 3: The same Spirit who breathed life into all creation empowers the baptized to bring about the reign of God in our midst. Jesus said: "The Spirit of the Lord is upon me because he has anointed me to bring glad tidings to the poor. He has sent me to proclaim liberty to captives and recovery of sight to the blind, to let the oppressed go free, and to proclaim a year acceptable to the Lord. Today this scripture passage is fulfilled in your hearing."

Reader 4: Gracious God, by water and the Holy Spirit you freed us from sin and gave us new life. Send your Holy Spirit upon us to be our Helper and Guide. Give us the spirit of wisdom and understanding, the spirit of right judgment and courage, the spirit of knowledge and reverence. Fill us with the spirit of wonder and awe in your presence. We ask this through Christ our Lord. Amen. (Adapted from the Rite of Confirmation, No. 25.)

Reader 5: Jesus promises to be with us always, to feed us with his life when we gather with him at table. He calls us together as one people, symbolized by the one loaf. The eucharist is the ultimate sign of who we are, one in Christ, and who we are called to be, one in love.

Reader 6: Dear God, thank you for counting us worthy to be in your presence and serve you. May we always be brought together in unity by the Holy Spirit. (Adapted from Eucharistic Prayer II.)

Resource 6

Jesus' Meal Ministry

How did the meal guests of Jesus feel . . .

The meal guests	before the meal?	during the meal?	after the meal?
The Five Thousand *Mark 6:34-44*			
Zacchaeus the Tax Collector *Luke 19:1-10*			
Levi *Mark 2:13-17*			
The Sinful Woman *Luke 7:36-50*			
Martha and Mary *Luke 10:38-42*			

Resource 7

Bread of Life

(based on John 6:22-69)

Narrator: It is the day after the multiplication of the loaves. Most of us were there yesterday. We were part of the crowd that Jesus fed with just five loaves of bread and two fish. We wanted to bring Jesus back with us to the city to make him our king, but he didn't want that. He went up into the mountain and hid from the crowd. Later that evening some of us saw his disciples leaving in the boat without him. This morning we've all gathered in the marketplace to see what new developments have happened. Everyone is still talking about the miracle of the bread and fish. Suddenly, Jesus arrives in the marketplace.

First Person: Here he comes now.

Second Person: How did he get across the lake? He didn't leave in the boat with his followers.

Third Person: I took the last boat home. He didn't come with me.

Fourth Person: (addressing Jesus) Sir, where did you disappear to yesterday? We were looking all over the mountainside for you.

Jesus (sadly) : Yes, you were looking for me. But only because I fed you. Not because you believed in me. You shouldn't be so concerned about perishable things like food. No, spend your energies seeking the eternal life that the Son of Man can give you. For God the Father has sent me for this very purpose.

Fifth Person: What do we have to do to please God?

Jesus: What God wants is this: that you believe in the one who has been sent to you.

Sixth Person: You must show us more miracles if you want us to believe in you.

First Person: Sure, just give us free bread every day, like our ancestors had while they journeyed in the wilderness.

Second Person: Yeah, like it says in the holy book, "Moses gave them bread from heaven."

Jesus: Moses didn't give it to them. My Father did. And now he offers you the true bread from heaven. The true bread is a person—the one sent by God from heaven, and he gives life to the world.

Third Person: Sir, if that's true, give us this bread every day of our lives.

Jesus: I am the bread of life. No one coming to me will every be hungry again. Those believing in me will never thirst.

Narrator: Then the Jews began murmuring and grumbling to themselves because he claimed to be the bread from heaven. (Everyone murmurs and grumbles.)

Fourth Person: What's he talking about? He is merely Jesus the son of Joseph. We know his father and mother; we know where he is from.

Fifth Person: What's he trying to say? We know he didn't come down from heaven.

Jesus: Don't talk among yourselves about my saying that. Those God speaks to, those who learn the truth from God, will understand. Yes, I am the bread of life. There was no real life in that bread from the skies which was given to your fathers in the wilderness, for they all died. But there is such a thing as bread from heaven that will give eternal life to everyone who eats it. And I am the living bread. Anyone who eats this bread will live forever; my flesh is this bread, given to the world.

Narrator: Then the Jews began arguing with each other about what he meant. (Everyone talks—some are getting angry.)

Sixth Person: How can this man give us his flesh to eat?

Jesus: With all the earnestness I possess I tell you this: Unless you eat the flesh of the son of man and drink his blood, you cannot have eternal life within you. My flesh is the true food, and my blood is the true drink. Everyone who eats my flesh and drinks my blood lives in me and I live in him.

First Person: This is very hard to understand.

Second Person: Who can tell what he means?

Third Person: This teaching is too hard.

Fourth Person: Who can listen to this?

Narrator: Jesus knew that his disciples were confused and some were grumbling and complaining.

Jesus: Some of you do not believe. That is what I meant when I said that no one can come to me unless God speaks to his or her heart.

Narrator: At this point many of his disciples turned away and did not follow him anymore. (Most of them turn away, shaking their heads in disgust. A few stay near Jesus.) Jesus watched them walk away. Then he turned to the Twelve.

Jesus: And you—are you going to leave me also?

Narrator: Peter answered for them all.

Peter: Master, to whom would we go? You alone have the words that give eternal life.
And we believe that you are the holy One of God.

Resource 8

"The Jesus Show" Questions

I think of the eucharist as my family's meal. What are some things your church can do to give the eucharist more of a family atmosphere?

I need leaders like priests, eucharistic ministers, lectors, singers, greeters, and active participants to serve at Mass. What role would you like to take in the future?

I really appreciate some of the things you tell me when you pray after receiving communion. Would you please tell the others what you say to me then?

I consider myself your friend. Tell me what I can do for you.

How did you understand my presence in the consecrated bread and wine when you made your first communion? How is your understanding different now?

Some of your friends do not know me very well. What can you do to help them to get to know me better?

Resource 9

Resource 9

You've heard many homilies in your life. I am interested to hear what was said in one of your favorite homilies to help you learn more about me.

During the sign of peace, I feel that I am really shaking hands or hugging you. When have you experienced the same thing when you have greeted a neighbor during that part of Mass?

Sometimes you look really intense when the priest says "This is my body. This is my blood." Other times you look more distracted. What are you thinking about during the consecration?

The priest is the leader of prayer at Mass. What can a priest do at Mass to help you to know me more intimately?

I still notice many people at Mass who do not come to the table and receive me in communion. What do you think I can do to reach out more to all people and convince them of the reconciliation present in the eucharist?

If you brought a friend who had never been to eucharist to a Mass at your parish, do you think this person would feel welcome? How can you help your parish to be more hospitable?

Eucharist Squares

Question 1

What is the rule for fasting before receiving communion?

Question 2

Is it permissible to take holy communion out of the church if you want to set up a tabernacle to worship the Blessed Sacrament in your home?

Question 3

What is the first day of the church's liturgical year?

Question 4

What is meant by the term "transubstantiation"?

Question 5

What are the two main parts of the Mass?

Question 6

What does *Kyrie Eleison* mean and what language is it in?

Question 7

What is the meaning of the term *viaticum*?

Question 8

Would a priest be able to consecrate a piece of sandwich bread into the body of Christ?

Question 9

During the part in the eucharistic prayer the priest offers a prayer for the bishop (for example, "for our bishop, Roger"). What happens when the bishop himself says Mass? What does he say when he gets to that part?

Question 10

What is an acolyte?

Question 11

What is the Sunday Mass schedule at this parish?

Question 12

Give an example of a memorial acclamation.

Question 13

Give three examples of holy days of obligation in the United States.

Question 14

What are the requirements for receiving first communion?

Question 15

What does *Agnus Dei* mean and what anguage is it?

Question 16

True or False. The second reading is always taken from one of the letters of St. Paul.

Question 17

What does "Amen" mean?

Question 18

During which seasons of the church year does the priest wear purple?

Question 19

From which of the four gospels will this year's readings be taken from?

Question 20

Where did the term "Mass" originate?

Resource 10

Eucharist Squares Answers

Question 1

What is the rule for fasting before receiving communion?

Correct: No food or water for one hour before receiving communion.

Bluff: No food or water after midnight on the day you are to receive communion.

Question 2

Is it permissible to take holy communion out of the church if you want to set up a tabernacle to worship the Blessed Sacrament in your home?

Correct: No, the Blessed Sacrament may only be displayed in churches or other specially designated chapels.

Bluff: A priest must first bless your home and approve of the tabernacle you are to use.

Question 3

What is the first day of the church's liturgical year?

Correct: The first Sunday of Advent.

Bluff: Christmas Day.

Question 4

What is meant by the term "transubstantiation"?

Correct: The doctrine that states that the bread and wine used at Mass are changed into the body and blood of Jesus.

Bluff: The doctrine that states that only a priest may celebrate Mass.

Question 5

What are the two main parts of the Mass?

Correct: The liturgy of the word and the liturgy of the eucharist.

Bluff: The offertory and the reception of communion.

Question 6

What does *Kyrie Eleis*on mean and what language is it in?

Correct: "Lord, have mercy." Greek.

Bluff: "The Lord be with you." Latin.

Question 7

What is the meaning of the term *viaticum?*

Correct: It is the final reception of holy communion before death.

Bluff: It is the church's governing body.

Question 8

Would a priest be able to consecrate a piece of sandwich bread into the body of Christ?

Correct: No. Only unleavened bread may be consecrated.

Bluff: Yes. As long as the priest recites the valid eucharistic prayer, any bread substance may be used for communion.

Question 9

During the part in the eucharistic prayer the priest offers a prayer for the bishop (for example, "for our bishop, Roger"). What happens when the bishop himself says Mass? What does he say when he gets to that part?

Correct: He says something like, "For me, your unworthy servant."

Bluff: He skips that part. To pray for himself would be considered lacking in humility.

Question 10

What is an acolyte?

Correct: An altar server.

Bluff: The leader of the choir.

Question 11

What is the Sunday Mass schedule at this parish?

Correct: (Give the exact correct times if you know them.)

Bluff: (Deliberately give at least one incorrect time.)

Question 12

Give an example of a memorial acclamation.

Correct: Dying you destroyed our death, rising you restored our live, Lord Jesus come in glory.

Bluff: Lamb of God, you take away the sins of the world, grant us peace.

Question 13

Give three examples of holy days of obligation in the United States.

Correct: New Year's Day, the Feast of the Assumption of Mary, and Christmas Day.

Bluff: The Feasts of the Immaculate Conception, the Annunciation, and the Assumption of Mary.

Question 14

What are the requirements for receiving first communion?

Correct: That you have a desire to receive and you know the difference between ordinary and blessed bread.

Bluff: That you have reached the age of reason and you have been instructed thoroughly into the meaning of holy eucharist.

Question 15

What does *Agnus Dei* mean and what language is it?

Correct: "Lamb of God," Latin.

Bluff: The Body of Christ, Greek.

Question 16

True or False. The second reading on Sunday is always taken from one of the letters of St. Paul.

Correct: False. It may be taken from any New Testament letter.

Bluff: True. During a course of one year, parts of each of Paul's letters are read.

Question 17

What does "Amen" mean?

Correct: "I agree" or "so be it."

Bluff: "Praise You, Lord."

Question 18

During which seasons of the church year does the priest wear purple?

Correct: Lent and Advent.

Bluff: Easter and Christmas.

Question 19

From which of the four gospels will this year's readings be taken from?

Correct: From the gospel of _________.

Bluff: The readings are equally distributed among the four gospels.

Question 20

Where did the term "Mass" originate?

Correct: From the Latin term *missa* which means "dismissal."

Bluff: Mass signifies the mass, or great amount, of followers gathered to worship Jesus Christ.

Resource 11

Reconciliation Speaker Preparation Sheet

Thank you for agreeing to speak with a group of teen-agers who are learning more about the sacrament of reconciliation.

Please plan to speak to the teens for about ten to fifteen minutes on several issues surrounding the practice and meaning of the sacrament. Here are some suggestions based on the material covered in this session:

- Teens often wonder why they have to go to confession, why they can't just ask God in their hearts for forgiveness. Please try to address that question for them.

- Teens sometimes worry about talking to the priest about something embarrassing, especially sexual sins. Can you address that worry for them?

- Teens wonder what happens after they go to confession and then happen to meet the priest later outside of the sacrament. Doesn't he remember all the person's sins?

- Please explain the seal of confession.

- Explain why the sacrament is known by many different names. See the resource from the *Catechism of the Catholic Church* on page 48 of the Participant Book for an outline.

- Teens sometimes believe that if they think something isn't a sin, then it isn't a sin. You may wish to expand on your definition of sin for them.

The teens have written other questions they wish to ask you. Please plan on a ten- to fifteen-minute question and answer period after your presentation.

Thank you.

Resource 12

Ordained Ministry Speaker Preparation Sheet

Thank you for agreeing to speak with the group of teenagers enrolled in a mini-course on sacraments. At the session you will attend, they will be learning about the sacrament of holy orders and about the vocation of ordained ministry. Please plan to speak with the group for about ten minutes. Here are some of the issues you might address:

- The occasion or "call" you experienced that led you to seek candidacy for ordination.

- A synopsis of your experience in the seminary, including things you most enjoyed along with things you disliked while there.

- Memories of your first year of ordained ministry.

- Some of the talents and gifts you bring to the faith community through your priesthood as well as some of the talents and gifts the faith community brings to you.

- The difficulties and rewards in keeping the vows you promised at ordination.

- An opinion on the future of your own ministry and on the shape of the priestly ministry in general for the church.

You may also be asked to respond to several questions the teens have about the sacrament of holy orders and the priesthood.

Resource 13

Scripture Prayer

Matthew 5:1-12	Matthew 5:13-16
Matthew 7:21, 24-25	Matthew 19:3-6
Matthew 22:35-40	Mark 10:6-9
John 2:1-11	John 15:9-12
John 15:12-16	John 17:20-23

Resource 14

Marriage Panel Preparation Sheet

Thank you for agreeing to be on a panel sharing some of your reflections, experiences, and history of your marriage and your relationship with your spouse. The teens you will be speaking to are concluding an eight-week mini-course on sacraments.

You will be on a panel with one or two other married couples. Please gear your comments to the special perspective you have according to the years you have been married. We have invited couples ranging in years married from newlywed to golden anniversary years!

The format of the panel discussion will be as follows:

Introduction

- Briefly introduce yourselves.
- Tell how you met.
- Tell something about your courtship.
- Tell how you became engaged.
- Tell something about your marriage preparation.
- Share one memorable part of your wedding day.

This part of your presentation should be about five or six minutes.

Issues

- How does God play a part in your relationship?
- What is the most difficult part of marriage?
- What is the most joyful part of marriage?

This part of your presentation should be about three or four minutes.

Questions

The final part of the panel discussion will be a question-and-answer segment. The teens have formed their own questions. Here are some samples:

- How did you know you had met the "right" person?
- How was the subject of marriage first brought up between the two of you?
- How do you handle serious arguments?
- Do you think there is an ideal age or time for two people to be married?
- Why is it important for you to get along with in-laws?
- Do you think your marriage reflects your family upbringing? How or how not?

Resource 15